Tolley's Capital G...
Post-Budget Sup...

D0581009

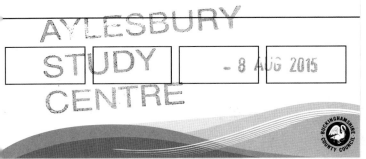

love your
library

Buckinghamshire Libraries
0845 230 3232
www.buckscc.gov.uk/libraries

---

24 hour renewal line
0303 123 0035

Tolley's Capital Gains Tax 2015 Post-Budget Supplement

by

Kevin Walton MA

Members of the LexisNexis Group worldwide

United Kingdom	LexisNexis, a Division of Reed Elsevier (UK) Ltd, Lexis House, 30 Farringdon Street, London EC4A 4HH, and London House, 20–22 East London Street, Edinburgh EH7 4BQ
Australia	LexisNexis Butterworths, Chatswood, New South Wales
Austria	LexisNexis Verlag ARD Orac GmbH & Co KG, Vienna
Benelux	LexisNexis Benelux, Amsterdam
Canada	LexisNexis Canada, Markham, Ontario
China	LexisNexis China, Beijing and Shanghai
France	LexisNexis SA, Paris
Germany	LexisNexis Deutschland GmbH, Munster
Hong Kong	LexisNexis Hong Kong, Hong Kong
India	LexisNexis India, New Delhi
Italy	Giuffrè Editore, Milan
Japan	LexisNexis Japan, Tokyo
Malaysia	Malayan Law Journal Sdn Bhd, Kuala Lumpur
Mexico	LexisNexis Mexico, Mexico
New Zealand	LexisNexis NZ Ltd, Wellington
Singapore	LexisNexis Singapore, Singapore
South Africa	LexisNexis Butterworths, Durban
USA	LexisNexis, Dayton, Ohio

© Reed Elsevier (UK) Ltd 2015

Published by Lexis Nexis
This is a Tolley title

ISBN for this volume: 9780754550624

Printed and bound in Great Britain by Hobbs the Printers Ltd, Totton, Hampshire

Visit LexisNexis at www.lexisnexis.co.uk

About This Supplement

This Supplement to Tolley's Capital Gains Tax 2014/15 gives details of changes in the law and practice of capital gains tax and corporation tax on chargeable gains from 2 July 2014 to 17 March 2015. It lists the changes in the same order and under the same paragraph headings as the annual publication. Also included is a summary of the Chancellor's Budget proposals.

Each time Tolley's Capital Gains Tax 2014/15 is used, reference should be made to the material contained in this Supplement. The Contents gives a list of all the chapters and paragraphs which have been updated.

Contents

Contents

Contents

1

Introduction

The charge to tax

[1.2] The paragraph after the bullet points is updated to read as follows.

'The scope of capital gains tax is to be extended to include disposals by non-UK residents of residential property in the UK. The new charge will apply with effect from April 2015. See **52.1** PRIVATE RESIDENCES.'

2

Annual Rates and Exemptions

Individuals — 2011/12 and subsequent years

[2.1] The third paragraph is updated to read as follows.

'Where the taxpayer's taxable income exceeds the basic rate limit so that part of his income is taxable at the higher rate or dividend upper rate (or, for 2016/17 onwards, the Scottish higher rate), the rate of capital gains tax is 28%. In other cases, the rate is 18% on any part of the gains that does not exceed the 'unused part of the basic rate band' for the year, and the 28% rate applies to any excess. Any gains which are charged to tax at 10% are treated for this purpose as the lowest part of the overall gains (so that the unused part of the basic rate band is set first against such gains).'

4

Anti-Avoidance

Accelerated payment notices

[4.34] The following is added at the end.

'HMRC have published a list of disclosed avoidance schemes likely to be subject to accelerated payment notices. See gov.uk/government/publications/tax-avoidance-schemes-on-which-accelerated-payments-may-be-charged-by-hmrc.'

5

Appeals

Settlement by agreement

[5.9] The following paragraph is added at the end.

'In *Foulser v HMRC* FTT, [2014] UKFTT 483 (TC); 2014 STI 2764 the taxpayer argued that he had sent a cheque to HMRC with a covering letter indicating that it was 'in full and final settlement' of his liability, and that since HMRC had cashed the cheque, this should be treated as a settlement by agreement of the appeal. The FTT rejected this contention.'

The hearing

[5.19] The following paragraph is added at the end.

'HMRC were prohibited by the First-tier Tribunal from citing an unpublished Special Commissioners' decision in *Ardmore Construction Ltd v HMRC* FTT, [2014] UKFTT 453 (TC); 2014 STI 2585.'

Judicial review

[5.35] A reference to *R (oao Derrin Brothers Properties Ltd) v HMRC (and related applications)* QB, [2014] STC 2238 is added at the end of the fourth paragraph.

6

Assessments

Discovery assessments

[6.9] The third paragraph from the end is amended to read as follows.

'In *Charlton v HMRC* UT, [2013] STC 866 it was held that the information provided with the taxpayer's return was sufficient to show that 'no officer could have missed the point that an artificial tax avoidance scheme had been implemented' and that 'on the basis of the information made available to him before the closure of the enquiry window, an officer would have been reasonably expected to have been aware of the insufficiency of tax such as to justify an assessment'; therefore, no discovery assessment was possible. It was not necessary that a hypothetical officer should have been able to comprehend all the workings of the scheme, or the legal and factual arguments that might arise, or be able to form a reasoned view of those matters. Discovery assessments in cases involving avoidance schemes were, however, upheld in *Smith v HMRC* FTT, [2013] UKFTT 368 (TC) and *Pattullo v HMRC (No 2)* FTT 2014, [2015] SFTD 24.'

7

Assets

Introduction

[7.1] The table is updated to read as follows.

Type of asset	Location
Assets held under alternative finance arrangements	3 ALTERNATIVE FINANCE ARRANGEMENTS
Derivative contracts of companies	15.8–15.13 COMPANIES — CORPORATE FINANCE AND INTANGIBLES
Bitcoin and other cryptocurrencies	7.12
Bookmakers' pitches	7.10
Business assets	36.2 HOLD-OVER RELIEFS; 58 ROLLOVER RELIEF
Domain names	7.11
Exempt assets	25.2–25.17 EXEMPTIONS AND RELIEFS
Furnished holiday accommodation	26 FURNISHED HOLIDAY ACCOMMODATION
Futures contracts	7.8
Government securities	28 GOVERNMENT SECURITIES
Image rights	7.13
Intangible fixed assets of companies	15.14, 15.15 COMPANIES — CORPORATE FINANCE AND INTANGIBLES
Know-how	7.4
Life insurance policies etc.	42 LIFE INSURANCE POLICIES AND DEFERRED ANNUITIES
Land	40 LAND
Loan relationships of companies	15.2–15.7 COMPANIES — CORPORATE FINANCE AND INTANGIBLES
Mineral royalties	46 MINERAL ROYALTIES
Options	7.7
Patents	7.5
Plant or machinery used for long funding lease	7.6
Private residences	52 PRIVATE RESIDENCES
Qualifying corporate bonds	53 QUALIFYING CORPORATE BONDS
Shares and securities	22 EMPLOYEE SHARE SCHEMES; 62 SHARES AND SECURITIES; 63 SHARES AND SECURITIES — IDENTIFICATION RULES; 65 SUBSTANTIAL SHAREHOLDINGS OF COMPANIES
Single payment scheme payment entitlement	7.14
Wasting assets	71 WASTING ASSETS

Milk quota

[7.9] The text is amended to read as follows.

'The milk quota system was introduced by the European Community in 1984 in order to regulate overall milk production (EC Council Regulation 856/84). Under the scheme, each member state was allocated a production quota. The national quota was then divided between all of the country's milk producers. If total UK production for any year exceeds the national quota then a levy is payable to the European Union by the Intervention Board (previously the Milk Marketing Board). This levy is then charged on to individual producers who have exceeded their own quota. Milk quota is to be abolished on 31 March 2015 (see further below).

Quota was originally allocated to milk producers in the UK by reference to levels of production for 1983 and was attached both to the producer and to the producer's land in use for milk production at 1 April 1984 (his 'holding'). Originally it was only possible to transfer milk quota permanently to another producer as part of a disposal of all or part of the holding to which it was attached (*SI 1984 No 1047*). This could be by outright sale of the land or by use of a scheme by which a permanent transfer of the quota is achieved by granting a short lease of the land. From 1 April 1994, it is possible in limited circumstances to sell milk quota without selling the land (*SI 1994 No 160*).

HMRC consider that milk quota is an asset separate from the land to which it is attached, and does not constitute an interest in or right over land. The decision in *Cottle v Coldicott* (Sp C 40), [1995] SSCD 239 supports this view. The taxpayer sold part of his quota using the scheme involving a short lease of land referred to above. The Special Commissioners held that the sale of milk quota amounted to the disposal of a separate asset. It was not a part disposal of the taxpayer's land, as he had contended, and neither were the proceeds a capital sum derived from the land within *TCGA 1992, s 22(1)* (see **10.2** CAPITAL SUMS DERIVED FROM ASSETS). Since the quota was a separate asset which had been allocated without cost in 1984, it followed that the allowable cost of acquisition was nil. The decision was followed in *Foxton v HMRC* (Sp C 485), [2005] SSCD 661.

For HMRC's view of the treatment of milk quota as a separate asset, see HMRC Capital Gains Manual CG77820. See also Revenue Tax Bulletin February 1993 pp 49–51 and December 1995 p 265. Where land and milk quota are acquired in a single transaction and the consideration is not allocated separately to each, an apportionment is required on a just and reasonable basis under *TCGA 1992, s 52(4)*.

For corporation tax purposes, milk quota is generally within the definition of an intangible fixed asset for the purposes of the intangible assets regime (see **15.14** COMPANIES — CORPORATE FINANCE AND INTANGIBLES). Broadly, milk quota acquired by a company from an unrelated party after 31 March 2002 is therefore outside the scope of corporation tax on chargeable gains (but see **15.14** COMPANIES — CORPORATE FINANCE AND INTANGIBLES for the detailed transitional provisions). A gain on disposal of milk quota not falling within that regime remains within the charge to corporation tax on chargeable gains (but see below as regards rollover relief).

Milk quota is a *fungible* asset, i.e. one which grows or diminishes as parts are acquired or disposed of but the individual parts of which cannot be separately identified. Acquisitions and disposals of quota are expressed in terms of a specific number of litres. Quota acquired in stages before 6 April 1998 formed a single asset for the purposes of both capital gains tax and corporation tax on chargeable gains. For the latter purposes, this treatment continues on and after that date (for acquisitions not falling within the corporation tax intangible assets regime — see above). Any quota allocated without cost on 1 April 1984 forms part of that asset but without contributing to its overall acquisition cost. Expenditure is allocated to a part disposal of the single asset in accordance with the formula in *TCGA 1992, s 42* (see **16.5** COMPUTATION OF GAINS AND LOSSES). For acquisitions and disposals on or after 6 April 2008, single asset treatment is reintroduced and the identification rules at **63.2** SHARES AND SECURITIES — IDENTIFICATION RULES apply. (HMRC Capital Gains Manual CG77901).

Abolition of milk quota

Milk quota is abolished with effect after 31 March 2015. Where a pool of milk quota is of negligible value, a negligible value claim (see **43.11** LOSSES) may be made to HMRC on or before that date. If no such claim is made there is a deemed disposal on the extinguishment of the asset resulting in an allowable loss equivalent to the amount incurred on acquiring the quota. See HMRC Brief 48/2014.

Tenant farmers

On the termination of a tenancy, the milk quota reverts to the landlord. The tenant and the landlord may agree compensation for the tenant's loss of milk quota. If not, the tenant is entitled to statutory compensation under *Agriculture Act 1986, s 13*. Where the compensation is paid under a contract, the time of the disposal is the time the contract is made. If the contract is conditional, it is the time the condition is satisfied. Where the compensation is statutory or is paid under a contractual agreement which does not provide for the reversion of the quota, the date of the disposal is the date of receipt of the compensation.

Tenant farmers require the consent of the landlord before selling milk quota. If the tenant makes a payment to the landlord in consideration of such consent the expenditure qualifies as a deduction in computing the chargeable gain on disposal of the milk quota. The landlord will have received a capital sum derived from an asset, taxable under *TCGA 1992, s 22(1)* (see **10.2** CAPITAL SUMS DERIVED FROM ASSETS).

(HMRC Capital Gains Manual CG77885, 77940).

Rollover relief etc.

For capital gains tax purposes, milk quota is a qualifying asset for rollover relief purposes (see **58.4** ROLLOVER RELIEF).

Milk quota is not regarded as a **71** WASTING ASSET (HMRC Capital Gains Manual CG77940). The rollover relief available for the exchange of joint interests in land also includes the parallel exchange of joint interests in milk quota (see **40.12** LAND).

Compensation payments

Compensation in respect of the temporary suspension of a proportion of quota is treated as a receipt of the farming trade, taxable as income. (HMRC Capital Gains Manual CG77920).

Compensation paid for a permanent reduction in milk quota is a capital sum derived from an asset, chargeable to capital gains tax under *TCGA 1992, s 22(1)* (see **10.2** CAPITAL SUMS DERIVED FROM ASSETS). (HMRC Capital Gains Manual CG77920 and Revenue Tax Bulletins May 1994 p 128, October 1997 p 474).

Bonus issue of Milk Marque shares to dairy farmers

In October 1998, milk producers who supplied Milk Marque Ltd in the year to 31 March 1998 were awarded a bonus consisting of preference shares (or in some cases loan stock) in the company. HMRC consider that the cost of acquisition of the shares or loan stock for capital gains tax purposes is equal to their nominal value. (Revenue Tax Bulletin August 1999 p 685).'

Image rights

[7.13] A new section is added as follows.

'For a discussion of the legal status and capital gains tax treatment of 'image rights' see HMRC Capital Gains Manual CG68405-68440.'

Single payment scheme payment entitlement

[7.14] A new section is added as follows.

'The EU single payment scheme for farmers ceased on 31 December 2014 and is replaced by a new basic payment scheme. The CGT treatment of single payment scheme payment entitlement is as follows.

Scotland, Wales and Northern Ireland

All single payment scheme payment entitlement ceased to exist on 31 December 2014. HMRC accept that payment entitlement became of negligible value on 16 May 2014 because 15 May 2014 was the last day that the entitlement must have been held in order for a person to establish that they were eligible for a payment under the scheme. Accordingly, a negligible value claim (see **43.11** LOSSES) may be made to HMRC on or before 31 December 2014. If no such claim is made, a deemed disposal occurs on the entitlement ceasing to exist (and an allowable loss may arise equal to the acquisition cost). HMRC do not accept that payment entitlement was of negligible value before 16 May 2014.

England

In England the choice was made to continue to use single payment scheme payment entitlement in the basic payment scheme. As a result, such entitlement has not become of negligible value and did not cease to exist on 31 December 2014.

(HMRC Brief 48/2014).

See also **58.4** ROLLOVER RELIEF.'

9

Assets held on 31 March 1982

Election for universal re-basing at 31 March 1982

[9.3] The final two paragraphs are amended to read as follows.

'In circumstances other than those covered by SP 4/92, HMRC may accept a late election by exercising its collection and management powers. In exercising those powers, HMRC adopt the same principles as they apply to late claims — see **66.1** TIME LIMITS — FIXED DATES. (HMRC Capital Gains Manual CG13800, 16780).

HMRC point out that in special cases elections need to be made by a person other than the person assessed. In the case of an assessment under *TCGA 1992, s 13* (charge on UK resident shareholder of an overseas resident company — see **48.7** OVERSEAS MATTERS), the election needs to be made by the company concerned. (HMRC Capital Gains Manual CG16760).'

11

Charities

Definition of charity

[11.2] The paragraph under the heading 'The jurisdiction condition' is amended to read as follows.

'The body or trust must be subject to the control of the High Court, Court of Session or High Court in Northern Ireland in the exercise of those courts' jurisdiction with respect to charities or of any other court in the exercise of a corresponding jurisdiction under the law of an EU member State or a territory specified in HMRC regulations (currently Iceland, Norway and Liechtenstein).'

13

Claims

Claim for recovery of overpaid tax

[13.7] The following paragraph is added before the final two paragraphs.

'The jurisdiction of the Tribunal in determining whether (i) above applies is limited to deciding whether the opinion of HMRC was 'unreasonable' in the judicial review sense. The Tribunal cannot consider afresh whether it would be unconscionable to seek to recover the tax or withhold repayment. See *Currie v HMRC* FTT 2014, [2015] SFTD 51.'

Claim for restitution of payment made under mistake of law

[13.8] The penultimate paragraph is amended to read as follows.

'In *Test Claimants in the FII Group Litigation v HMRC* CJEU, [2014] STC 638 *FA 2007, s 107* above was held to breach European Community law because it does not incorporate any transitional provisions. The exception in (c) above was introduced by *FA 2014, s 299* to amend *FA 2007, s 107* to comply with that decision. Although the exception takes legal effect on 17 July 2014 (the date of Royal Assent to *FA 2014*), it applies to actions brought, and causes of action arising, before, on or after that date. See also *United Kingdom v European Commission* CJEU, (C-640/13); 2015 STI 52, which confirmed that *FA 2007, s 107* breached EU law (but note that the decision did not consider the changes made by *FA 2014*).'

14

Companies

Capital gains tax charge on high value disposals of dwellings

[14.10] The three paragraphs before the heading 'Restriction of losses' are replaced by the following.

'*FA 2014, ss 109, 110* extend ATED to include dwellings valued at more than £1 million with effect from 1 April 2015 and to include dwellings valued at more than £500,000 with effect from 1 April 2016. The CGT threshold amount will be amended in line with these changes. (Tax Information and Impact Note 'Capital gains tax: changes to the threshold amount for ATED-related CGT', 10 December 2014).

A disposal made by the company in the six years ending with the day of the disposal in question (but not before 6 April 2013) is a '*related disposal*' if it meets conditions (a)–(c) above and the single-dwelling interest in (c) above is either the same interest or another single-dwelling interest in the same dwelling.

[*TCGA 1992, ss 2B–2D, 4(3A); FA 2013, Sch 25 paras 4, 5*].'

Reconstructions involving transfer of business

[14.11] The reference to HMRC Capital Gains Manual in the third paragraph is updated to CG52720–52728.

15

Companies — Corporate Finance and Intangibles

Loan relationships

[15.2] The following paragraph is added at the end.

'A number of changes are to be made to the loan relationships regime, broadly with effect for accounting periods beginning on or after 1 January 2016. The intention is to make the rules more certain and easier to comply with by clarifying the structure and detailed rules, and to make the regime fairer by providing more robust protection against tax avoidance. See www.gov.uk/government/publications/corporation-tax-modernising-the-taxation-of-corporate-debt-and-derivative-contracts.'

Summary of provisions

[15.3] References to *SI 2014 Nos 3188, 3325* are added to the list of statutory references at the end.

Derivative contracts

[15.8] The following paragraph is added at the end.

'A number of changes are to be made to the derivative contracts regime, broadly with effect for accounting periods beginning on or after 1 January 2016. The intention is to make the rules more certain and easier to comply with by clarifying the structure and detailed rules, and to make the regime fairer by providing more robust protection against tax avoidance. See www.gov.uk/government/publications/corporation-tax-modernising-the-taxation-of-corporate-debt-and-derivative-contracts.'

20

Disclosure of Tax Avoidance Schemes

Disclosure regime

[20.2] The following is added after the second paragraph.

'Legislation in Finance Bill 2015 will strengthen the regime by updating the rules determining what has to be disclosed to ensure avoidance that is being marketed and used now is disclosed; changing the information that must be provided to HMRC; enabling HMRC to publish information about promoters and disclosed schemes; and establishing a taskforce to enforce the strengthened regime.

- Promoters will be required to notify HMRC within 30 days if the name of a scheme, or the name or address of a promoter, changes after a reference number has been issued.
- Employers will be required to provide HMRC with prescribed information (under SI 2012/1836) about each employee to whom they have provided information in relation to notifiable arrangements.
- New provisions will enable HMRC to require a person suspected of being an introducer in relation to a notifiable proposal to provide prescribed information about those with whom they have made a marketing contact.
- Changes will be made to provide that no duty of confidentiality or other restriction on disclosure (however imposed) can prevent persons from being able to voluntarily provide information or documents to HMRC which they suspect may assist HMRC in determining whether there has been a breach of any of the DOTAS requirements.
- HMRC will be able to publish information about promoters and schemes that are notified under the DOTAS regime and which have been issued with a reference number. HMRC must inform a promoter before publishing any information which would identify that person as a promoter to give them an opportunity to make representations about publication, and may not publish any information that will identify scheme users. HMRC will be required to publish information about court rulings that are relevant to earlier publication under this provision.
- The penalties for users of tax avoidance schemes who fail to correctly provide information about the reference number etc. to HMRC are increased from an amount not exceeding £100, £500, and £1,000 (depending on the circumstances) to an amount not exceeding £5,000, £7,500 and £10,000 respectively.
- The period during which HMRC may issue a scheme reference number will be increased from 30 to 90 days.

The provisions will apply on or after the date that the Finance Act 2015 receives Royal Assent. Certain transitional will provisions apply. See www.gov.uk/government/publications/disclosure-of-tax-avoidance-schemes.'

High-risk promoters of avoidance schemes

[20.6] The section is replaced by the following.

'With effect from 17 July 2014, a special compliance regime applies to promoters of tax avoidance schemes who satisfy one or more 'threshold conditions' relating to previous behaviour. The regime provides for the issuing of a 'conduct notice' (see **20.9** below) requiring the person to whom it is given to comply with specified conditions as to the information they provide to clients, compliance with any disclosure requirements under the provisions at **20.2** onwards above and not promoting schemes which rely on contrived or abnormal steps to produce a tax advantage. Promoters who fail to comply with a conduct notice may be issued with a monitoring notice (see **20.10** below). Names of promoters subject to such a notice may be published by

HMRC, including details of how the conduct notice was breached, and promoters are required to notify their monitored status to clients. Information powers and penalties apply to promoters subject to a conduct notice and to promoters subject to a monitoring notice and their clients and intermediaries. Clients who fail to comply with their duty to provide HMRC with a monitored promoter's reference number are subject to extended time limits for assessment (see **6.12** ASSESSMENTS). Special rules apply to partnerships — see **20.15** below.

The taxes covered by the provisions are income tax, capital gains tax, corporation tax, petroleum revenue tax, inheritance tax, stamp duty land tax, stamp duty reserve tax and annual tax on enveloped dwellings. [*FA 2014, s 283(1)*].

For HMRC guidance on the provisions see www.gov.uk/government/uploads /system/uploads/attachment_data/file/403423/Promoters_of_Tax_Avoidance_ Schemes_Guidance.pdf.

A number of changes to the provisions are to be made in the Finance Bill 2015.

- HMRC will be able to issue conduct notices to a broader range of connected persons under the common control of a promoter of tax avoidance schemes.
- The three year time limit for issuing notices to promoters who have failed to disclose avoidance schemes to HMRC under the provisions at **20.2** onwards above will apply from the date when the failure comes to the attention of HMRC rather than the date of the underlying failure.
- A new threshold condition will be introduced for failing to comply with National Insurance contributions disclosure requirements.
- Changes will be made to ensure that the threshold conditions take account of decisions by independent bodies in matters of all relevant forms of professional misconduct.

The changes will apply with effect from the date of Royal Assent to the Finance Act 2015. See www.gov.uk/government/publications/promoters-of-tax-avoida nce-schemes--2.

Definitions

[20.7] Arrangements are subject to the provisions if they enable, or might be expected to enable, any person to obtain a 'tax advantage' and the main benefit, or one of the main benefits, that might be expected to arise from the arrangements is the obtaining of that advantage. '*Arrangements*' include any agreement, scheme, arrangement or understanding of any kind, whether or not legally enforceable, involving one or more transactions.

A proposal is subject to the provisions if it is a proposal for arrangements which, if entered into, would be subject to the provisions (whether the proposal relates to a particular person or to any person who may seek to use it).

A '*tax advantage*' includes relief or increased relief from tax, repayment or increased repayment of tax, avoidance or reduction of a charge or assessment to tax, avoidance of a possible assessment to tax, deferral of a payment, or advancement of a repayment, of tax and avoidance of an obligation to deduct or account for tax.

A person carrying on a business in the course of which he is, or has been, a promoter in relation to a proposal or arrangements carries on that business 'as a promoter'. A person is a *'promoter'* in relation to a proposal if he:

(i)   is to any extent responsible for the design of the proposed arrangements; or

(ii)   makes a 'firm approach' to another person with a view to making the proposal available for implementation by that, or any other, person; or

(iii)   makes the proposal available for implementation by other persons.

A person is a *'promoter'* in relation to arrangements if he:

(a)   is a promoter by virtue of (ii) or (iii) above in relation to a proposal which is implemented by the arrangements; or

(b)   is to any extent responsible for the design, organisation or management of the arrangements.

A company is not, however, a promoter if the only persons to whom it provides services in connection with a proposal or arrangements are companies in the same group, provided that it has not provided such services to any person other than a group member during the three previous years. If the company subsequently provides such services to a person other than a group member, this rule is deemed not to have applied during the previous three years. Companies are members of the same group for this purpose if one is a 51% subsidiary of the other or both are 51% subsidiaries of a third company.

A person is not a promoter on account of (i) above or by virtue of being responsible for the design of arrangements within (b) above, if either he does not provide any tax advice in connection with the arrangements or could not reasonably be expected to know that the arrangements or proposal are subject to the provisions.

Where a promoter (a *'monitored promoter'*) of a proposal is subject to a monitoring notice (see **20.10** below), the proposal is a *'monitored proposal'* if the promoter, on or after the date the notice takes effect:

•   first makes a firm approach to another person about the proposal;

•   first makes the proposal available for implementation by another person; or

•   first becomes aware of any transaction forming part of the proposed arrangements being entered into by any person.

Where a promoter of arrangements is a monitored promoter, the arrangements are *'monitored arrangements'* if:

•   the promoter is a promoter of a proposal implemented by the arrangements by virtue of (ii) or (iii) above and, on or after the date the notice takes effect he:

    –   first makes a firm approach to another person about the proposal;

    –   first makes the proposal available for implementation by another person; or

    –   first becomes aware of any transaction forming part of the proposed arrangements being entered into by any person; or

- the date on which the promoter first takes part in designing, organising or managing the arrangements is on or after the date on which the notice takes effect; or
- the arrangements enable, or are likely to enable, the person entering into the transactions forming them to obtain the tax advantage on or after the date the notice takes effect.

A person makes a '*firm approach*' to another person if he provides information about the proposal, including an explanation of the expected tax advantage, at a time when the proposed arrangements have been 'substantially designed', with a view to that, or any other, person entering into transactions forming part of the proposed arrangements. Arrangements have been '*substantially designed*' when it would be reasonable to believe that a person wishing to obtain the tax advantage might use the scheme or a scheme which is not substantially different.

A person is an '*intermediary*' in relation to a proposal if he is not a promoter of it but he communicates information about it to another person in the course of a business with a view to that, or any other, person entering into transactions forming part of the proposed arrangements.

'*Prescribed*' means prescribed, or of a description prescribed, in regulations made by HMRC by statutory instrument.

A person ('P') is a '*controlling member*' of a partnership (see **20.15** below) at any time when P has a right to a share of more than half the assets or income of the partnership. Any interests or rights of any individual who is connected with P (if P is an individual) and of any body corporate controlled by P are attributed to P for this purpose. The following are connected with P: P's spouse or civil partner; P's relatives (i.e. a brother, sister, ancestor or lineal descendant); the spouse or civil partner of P's relatives; relatives of P's spouse or civil partner; and the spouse or civil partner of a relative of P's spouse or civil partner. P controls a body corporate if P has power to secure that its affairs are conducted in accordance with P's wishes either by means of holding shares or voting power in a body corporate (whether or not the body corporate in question) or as a result of powers under the articles of association or other document regulating a body corporate.

A '*managing partner*' of a partnership is a member of the partnership who directs, or is on a day to day level in control of, the management of the partnership's business.

The Treasury may amend the definitions of 'controlling member' and 'managing partner' by statutory instrument.

An '*authorised HMRC officer*' is an HMRC officer who is, or is a member of a class of officers who are, authorised by the Commissioners for HMRC for the purposes of the high-risk promoter provisions.

[*FA 2014, ss 234–236, 254, 282, 283, Sch 36 paras 19–21; SI 2015 No 130*].

Threshold conditions

[20.8] A person meets a threshold condition if:

(a)   HMRC publish information about the person under the deliberate tax defaulter provisions in *FA 2009, s 94* (see **31.3** HMRC — CONFIDENTIALITY OF INFORMATION);

(b)   the person is named in a report under *FA 2014, s 285* because HMRC have determined that the person has breached the Code of Practice on Taxation for Banks by promoting arrangements which they cannot reasonably have believed achieved a tax result intended by Parliament;

(c)   the person has been given a conduct notice under the dishonest conduct of tax agents provisions in *FA 2012, Sch 38 para 4* (see **34.11** HMRC INVESTIGATORY POWERS) and either the time limit for making an appeal against the notice has expired or an appeal has been made and rejected by the Tribunal;

(d)   the person fails to comply with disclosure requirements under *FA 2004, ss 308–310, 313ZA* (see **20.3** above), including where the person had a reasonable excuse for non-compliance;

(e)   the person is charged with a specified criminal offence (but such a charge is disregarded for this purpose if it has been dismissed, if the proceedings have been discontinued or following final acquittal);

(f)   arrangements of which the person is a promoter have been subject to one or more opinion notices of the GAAR Advisory Panel (see **4.4** ANTI-AVOIDANCE) that the arrangements are not reasonable and those notices, taken together, state the opinion of at least two of the members of the sub-panel considering the arrangements;

(g)   a specified professional body determines that the person is guilty of misconduct, or a breach of a rule or condition imposed by the body, which relates to the provision of tax advice or tax related services, refers the misconduct or breach to a disciplinary process or a conciliation, arbitration or similar settlement process, and imposes a prescribed penalty (including a fine greater than £5,000, suspension or expulsion);

(h)   the Financial Conduct Authority, Financial Services Authority or another prescribed regulatory body imposes a prescribed sanction for misconduct (including a fine or suspension of approval);

(i)   the person fails to comply with an information notice under *FA 2008, Sch 36 paras 1, 2, 5 or 5A* (see **34.4** HMRC INVESTIGATORY POWERS);

(j)   the person ('P') enters into an agreement with another person ('C') which relates to a proposal or arrangements of which P is the promoter on terms which impose certain contractual obligations on C (see further below); or

(k)   the person has been given a 'stop notice' and, after the end of the period of 30 days beginning on the day the notice is given, makes a firm approach to another person with a view to making an 'affected proposal' (i.e. a proposal which is in substance the same as the proposal specified in the stop notice) available for implementation by that person or another or makes an affected proposal available for implementation by other persons.

For the purposes of (e) above, the following offences are specified:

•   a common law offence of cheating the public revenue;

•   in Scotland, an offence of fraud or uttering;

- an offence under *Theft Act 1968, s 17* (false accounting) or NI equivalent;
- an offence under *TMA 1970, s 106A* (fraudulent evasion of income tax);
- an offence under *TMA 1970, s 107* (false statements: Scotland);
- an offence under *Customs and Excise Management Act 1979, s 50(2)* (improper importation of goods with intent to defraud or evade duty), *s 167* (untrue declarations etc.), *s 168* (counterfeiting documents etc.), *s 170* (fraudulent evasion of duty) or *s 170B* (taking steps for the fraudulent evasion of duty);
- an offence under *VATA 1994, s 72(1)* (being knowingly concerned in the evasion of VAT), *s 72(3)* (false statement etc.), or *s 72(8)* (conduct involving commission of other offence);
- an offence under *Fraud Act 2006, s 1*;
- an offence under *CRCA 2005, s 30* (impersonating a Commissioner or officer of HMRC), *s 31* (obstruction of HMRC officer etc.) or *s 32* (assault of HMRC officer);
- an offence under *SI 2007 No 2157, Reg 45(1)* (money laundering); and
- an offence under *Criminal Justice and Licensing (Scotland) Act 2010, s 49(1)* (possession of articles for use in fraud).

In (g) above, the specified professional bodies are the Institutes of Chartered Accountants in England and Wales and of Scotland, the General Council of the Bar, the Faculty of Advocates, the General Council of the Bar in Northern Ireland, the Law Society, the Law Societies of Scotland and Northern Ireland, the Association of Accounting Technicians, the Association of Chartered Certified Accountants, the Association of Taxation Technicians and any other prescribed body.

The threshold condition in (j) above is met if the contractual obligation prevents or restricts the disclosure by C to HMRC of information about the proposals or arrangements, whether or not by referring to a wider class of persons, or if the obligation requires C to impose a similar contractual obligation on any tax advisor to whom C discloses information. The condition is also met if contractual obligations require C:

- to meet the whole or part of the costs of, or contribute to a fund to meet the costs of, any 'proceedings' relating to arrangements promoted by C (whether or not implemented by C) or, where C implements the arrangements, to take out an insurance policy to insure against the risk of having to meet such costs; and
- to obtain P's consent before making any agreement with HMRC regarding arrangements promoted by P or withdrawing or discontinuing any appeal against a decision about such arrangements.

'*Proceedings*' for this purpose include any sort of proceedings for resolving disputes (i.e. not just court proceedings) which are commenced or contemplated.

Note that, where the threshold condition in question is within (i) above, it is treated as met when the time limit for compliance with the information notice expires without the promoter complying with it.

Where a threshold condition within (a), (c) or (e)–(i) above is met by a person who is a controlling member or managing partner of a partnership and HMRC subsequently make a determination as to whether a conduct notice (see **20.9** below) should be given to the partnership, then, if the person is still a controlling member or managing partner of the partnership, the partnership is treated as meeting the threshold condition at the earlier time (whether or not the partnership was bound by the act or omission in question).

Stop notices

An authorised HMRC officer may give a person ('P') a *'stop notice'* (see (k) above) if:

- a person has been given a follower notice (see **4.30** ANTI-AVOIDANCE) relating to particular arrangements;
- P is a promoter of a proposal implemented by those arrangements; and
- 90 days have passed since the follower notice was given, the notice has not been withdrawn and, if representations objecting to the notice were made, HMRC have confirmed the notice.

A stop notice must specify the arrangements which are the subject of the follower notice, specify the court or tribunal ruling identified in that notice, specify the proposal implemented by those arrangements and explain the effect of the stop notice. An authorised HMRC officer may notify P in writing that a stop notice is to cease to have effect from a specified date (which may be before the notice is given).

Companies etc.

If a threshold condition within (a), (c) or (e)–(i) above is met by a person at a time (the 'earlier time') when he has control of a body corporate and a determination under **20.9** below is made in relation to the body corporate at a later time, then, if the person has control of the body corporate at that later time, the body corporate is treated as having met the threshold condition at the earlier time. For this purpose, a person has control of a body corporate if he has power to secure that the affairs of the body are conducted in accordance with his wishes, either by means of holding shares or possessing voting power in that, or any other, body corporate or as a result of any powers under the articles of association or other document regulating that, or any other, body corporate.

The Treasury may amend the above provisions by statutory instrument.

[*FA 2014, Sch 34, Sch 36 para 4; SI 2015 No 131*].

Conduct notices

[20.9] A *'conduct notice'* is a notice requiring the person to whom it is given to comply with specified conditions. An authorised HMRC officer must issue a conduct notice if he becomes aware at any time that a person carrying on a business as a promoter has, in the previous three years and at a time when he was carrying on such a business, met one or more of the threshold conditions (see **20.8** above) and the officer determines that the meeting of the condition or conditions should be regarded as significant in view of the purposes of the high-risk promoter regime. For this purpose, meeting any of the threshold conditions in **20.8**(a)–(c), (e) or (f) is automatically treated as significant. No conduct notice need be issued if the officer determines that it is inappropriate to do so, having regard to the extent of the impact that the promoter's activities are likely to have on the collection of tax. A conduct notice cannot be issued if the promoter is already subject to such a notice or to a monitoring notice (see **20.10** below). A conduct notice given to a partnership must state that it is a partnership conduct notice.

The terms of a conduct notice are determined by the officer giving it, but are limited to conditions that it is reasonable to impose to ensure that the promoter:

(a)   provides adequate information (as defined, and including an assessment of the risk that the expected tax advantage will not be achieved) to clients (as defined) about proposals and arrangements of which he is a promoter;

(b)   provides adequate information to intermediaries about proposals of which he is a promoter;

(c)   does not fail to comply with any specified duties under the disclosure of tax avoidance schemes provisions (see **20.2** above) or under *FA 2008, Sch 36 paras 1–9* (see **34.4** HMRC INVESTIGATORY POWERS);

(d)   does not discourage others from complying with any specified disclosure obligation;

(e)   does not enter into an agreement which imposes on another person contractual obligations within **20.8**(j) above;

(f)   does not promote proposals or arrangements which rely on, or involve a proposal to rely on, one or more contrived or abnormal steps to produce a tax advantage; and

(g)   does not fail to comply with any stop notice (see **20.8** above).

In the case of a partnership conduct notice, conditions may be imposed relating to the persons who are partners when the notice is given and to persons who subsequently become partners.

Before deciding on the terms of a notice, the officer must provide an opportunity for the promoter to comment on the proposed terms.

A conduct notice has effect from the date specified in it and may be amended at any time by an authorised HMRC officer. A notice ceases to have effect after two years or on an earlier date specified in the notice. It also ceases to have effect if a monitoring notice (see **20.10** below) takes effect. A notice may also be withdrawn by an authorised HMRC officer.

[*FA 2014, ss 237–241, Sch 36 para 5*].

Information

HMRC may (as often as is necessary) by notice in writing require a person subject to a conduct notice to provide information or produce a document which is reasonably required for the purpose of monitoring compliance with the notice. [*FA 2014, s 262*].

Monitoring notices

[20.10] If an authorised HMRC officer determines that a promoter has failed to comply with one or more conditions in a conduct notice, he must apply to the Tribunal for approval to give the promoter a 'monitoring notice', unless the conditions in question were imposed under **20.9**(a)–(c) above and the officer considers the failure to comply to be such a minor matter that it should be disregarded. An application for approval must include a draft notice and the officer must also notify the promoter of the application. The notice to the promoter must state which conditions have not been complied with and the officer's reasons for determining that there has been a failure to comply.

The Tribunal may approve the giving of a monitoring notice only if it is satisfied that the officer would be justified in giving it and that the promoter has been given a reasonable opportunity to make representations to the Tribunal. If the promoter's representations include a statement that it was not reasonable to include a particular condition in the conduct notice and the Tribunal is satisfied that it was not so reasonable, the Tribunal must assume that there was no failure to comply with the condition (and must refuse HMRC's application if this applies to all the conditions which HMRC consider have not been complied with). If the Tribunal gives approval it may amend the draft notice. A promoter may appeal against the decision of the Tribunal in the usual way (see 5 APPEALS).

A monitoring notice must explain its effect and specify the date from which it takes effect (which cannot be earlier than the date the notice is given). It must also inform the recipient of the right to request its withdrawal (see further below). The notice must state the conditions of the conduct notice which HMRC have determined that the promoter has failed to comply with and the reasons for that determination. A notice given to a partnership must state that it is a partnership monitoring notice. If the notice is a replacement notice given to a former partner of a partnership itself subject to a monitoring notice (see **20.15** below) it must also state the date of that notice and the name of the partnership.

Withdrawal of a monitoring notice

An authorised HMRC officer may withdraw a notice if he thinks it is no longer necessary, taking into account matters including the promoter's behaviour and compliance whilst the notice has had effect and likely future behaviour.

A person subject to a monitoring notice (a *'monitored promoter'*) may make a request in writing to an authorised HMRC officer that the notice should cease to apply. Such a request can be made at any time after the twelve months beginning with the end of the period in which an appeal against the Tribunal's decision to approve the giving of the notice could have been made or, where such an appeal was made, the twelve months beginning with the date on which the appeal was finally determined, withdrawn or otherwise disposed of. If the notice is a replacement notice, the twelve-month period applies by reference to appeals against the Tribunal's decision about the original notice. HMRC must determine whether or not the notice should cease to apply within the 30 days beginning with the date on which the request is received and must notify the promoter of their determination specifying the date from which the notice is to cease to apply (and whether or not a follow-on conduct notice – see below – is to be given) or their reasons for refusal of the request.

A monitored promoter can appeal against a refusal by HMRC by notice in writing within 30 days beginning with the date on which the refusal notice was given, stating the grounds of appeal.

If HMRC decide to withdraw a notice or, following a request from the promoter, decide that a notice should cease to apply, they may issue a follow-on conduct notice to take effect immediately after the monitoring notice ceases to have effect.

[FA 2014, ss 242–247, Sch 36 para 6].

Effects of a monitoring notice

[20.11] A monitoring notice has the following effects.

Publication by HMRC

HMRC may publish the name (including business name and any previous name or pseudonym) of a monitored promoter together with the business address or registered office, the nature of the business carried on, a statement of the conditions in a conduct notice with which the promoter has failed to comply and any other information which they consider appropriate to publish to make clear the promoter's identity. Where the monitored promoter is a partnership, it is the details of the partnership which may be published (and not those of particular partners). Publication may not take place before the end of the period in which an appeal against the Tribunal's decision to approve the giving of the notice can be made or, where such an appeal is made, before the appeal is finally determined, withdrawn or otherwise disposed of. If the notice is a replacement notice (see 20.15 below), the restriction applies by reference to appeals against the Tribunal's decision about the original notice. If HMRC publish details of a monitored promoter they must publish the fact of a withdrawal of the notice in the same way. [FA 2014, s 248, Sch 36 para 14].

Publication by monitored promoter

The monitored promoter must give a notice stating that he is a monitored promoter and which conduct notice conditions have not been complied with to anyone who is a client (as defined) at the time the monitoring notice takes effect and to anyone who becomes a client whilst the notice has effect. The notice must also identify the original monitoring notice if the monitoring notice in question is a replacement notice (see 20.15 below). The information in the notice must also be published in a prominent position on the promoter's website and any other websites promoting, or providing informa-tion on, the activities of the promoter. The requirement to give such notices does not apply until ten days after the end of the period in which an appeal against the Tribunal's decision to approve the giving of the notice can be made or, where such an appeal is made, ten days after the appeal is finally determined, withdrawn or otherwise disposed of. If the notice is a replacement notice (see **20.15** below), the requirement applies by reference to appeals against the Tribunal's decision about the original notice. In the case of someone becoming a client whilst the monitoring notice has effect, the promoter must give them the required notice within ten days of their first becoming a client.

The information, together with the promoter's reference number (see below), must also be included in certain publications and correspondence with clients and intermediaries and in correspondence with professional bodies and regulatory authorities.

[FA 2014, s 249; SI 2015 No 549, Regs 2, 3].

Reference number

Once all rights to appeal against the decision of the Tribunal to approve the giving of the monitoring notice (or original notice) are exhausted, HMRC will allocate a reference number to the monitored promoter. HMRC then notify the number to the promoter or, if the promoter is non-UK resident, to any person who HMRC know is an intermediary in relation to a proposal of the promoter. A promoter so notified must in turn notify the number to anyone who becomes a client while the monitoring notice has effect or who is an intermediary whilst the notice has effect. Unless the monitoring notice is a replacement notice, he must also notify the number to any person he can reasonably be expected to know has entered into arrangements, in the period in which the conduct notice preceding the monitoring notice had effect, which are likely to enable that person to obtain a tax advantage whilst the monitoring notice has effect if the monitored promoter is a promoter of those arrangements or of a proposal implemented by those arrangements. Notification must be given within 30 days of HMRC's notification of the number or later event triggering the requirement to notify.

An intermediary who is notified by HMRC of a reference number or a person so notified by a promoter must, within 30 days of being so notified, provide the number to any other person they might reasonably be expected to know has become, or is likely to have become, a client of the monitored promoter whilst the monitoring notice has had effect. An intermediary must also, within 30 days, provide the number to any person to whom he has communicated, in the course of a business and since the monitoring notice took effect, information about a proposal of the monitored promoter and to any person who he might reasonably be expected to know has, since the notice took effect, entered into, or is likely to enter into, transactions forming part of arrangements of which the monitored promoter is a promoter. An intermediary or other person notified of a reference number by the promoter does not have to provide the number to a person if he reasonably believes that that person has already been provided with the number.

A person who has been notified of a reference number under any of the above provisions must report it to HMRC if he expects to obtain a tax advantage from arrangements of which the promoter to whom the number relates is a promoter. The report must normally be made in each tax return for any period which includes a period for which the tax advantage is obtained (irrespective of whether the return relates to the tax affected). If no tax return has to be made for such periods or if a tax return is not submitted by the filing date, a separate report must be made by 31 January following the end of each tax year in which a tax advantage may arise (or, for corporation tax purposes, not later than twelve months from the end of each accounting period in which a tax advantage may arise) to HMRC, Counter Avoidance Directorate CA Intelligence SO528, PO Box 194 Bootle L69 9AA. If the arrangements give rise to a claim under *TCGA 1992, s 261B* (trade loss treated as CGT loss — see **43.21** LOSSES) and that claim is made outside of a tax return, the claim must include the reference number.

[*FA 2014, ss 250–253; SI 2015 No 549, Regs 5, 6, Sch 2*].

Information

The following information powers apply where a monitoring notice has effect.

Information and documents

HMRC may by notice in writing require a monitored promoter or a person who is an intermediary in relation to a monitored proposal (see **20.7** above) to provide information or produce a document which is reasonably required by HMRC for:

- considering the possible consequences of implementing a monitored proposal for the tax positions of those implementing it;
- checking the tax position of any person that HMRC believe has implemented a monitored proposal;
- checking the tax position of any person that HMRC believe has entered into transactions forming monitored arrangements.

A notice can be given to an intermediary only after he has been notified of the promoter's reference number. A notice given for the purpose of checking the tax position of a person cannot be given more than four years after that person's death. '*Checking*' and '*tax position*' are defined as for HMRC's general information powers (see **34.3** HMRC INVESTIGATORY POWERS) but a person's tax position also includes his position as regards deductions or repayments of tax, or sums representing tax, that he is required to make under PAYE regulations or other provisions and the withholding by him of another person's PAYE income (within *ITEPA 2003, s 683*).

Information or a document required under a notice must be provided or produced within ten days beginning with the day the notice is given or within such longer period as HMRC direct.

The giving of a notice under the above provisions must be approved by the Tribunal if it requires a promoter or intermediary to provide information or produce a document relating (wholly or partly) to a person who is not that promoter or intermediary and not an 'undertaking' of which the promoter or intermediary is the 'parent undertaking'. The promoter or intermediary must normally have been told that the information or documents are required and have been given a reasonable opportunity to make representations to HMRC, but is not entitled to be present at the hearing. The Tribunal must be given a summary of any representations made. Where the Tribunal is satisfied that informing the promoter or intermediary would prejudice the assessment or collection of tax, it can approve the giving of the notice without the taxpayer having been informed. There is no right of appeal against a decision of the Tribunal. '*Undertaking*' and '*parent undertaking*' are defined as in *Companies Act 2006, ss 1161, 1162, Sch 7*.

[*FA 2014, ss 255, 256*].

Ongoing duty to provide information

HMRC may give a notice to a monitored promoter requiring him to provide prescribed information and produce prescribed documents relating to all monitored proposals and monitored arrangements of which he is a promoter at the time of the notice or of which he becomes a promoter after that time but before the monitoring notice ceases to have effect. A notice must specify the time within which information must be provided or a document produced. [*FA 2014, s 257*]. See *SI 2015 No 549, Reg 7* for the prescribed information and documents.

Person dealing with non-resident monitored promoter

Where a non-UK resident monitored promoter fails to comply with a duty to provide information under either of the above powers, HMRC may issue a notice requiring the information from:

(1)   a person who is an intermediary in relation to the monitored proposal concerned;

(2)   a person to whom the promoter has made a firm approach with a view to making the proposal available for implementation by a third person;

(3)   where HMRC are not aware of any person within (1) or (2) above to whom a notice could be given, a person who has implemented the proposal in question; or

(4)   where the duty in question relates to monitored arrangements, a person who has entered into any transaction forming part of those arrangements.

The HMRC officer giving the notice must reasonably believe that the person to whom the notice is given is able to provide the information. Information required under a notice must be provided within ten days beginning with the day the notice is given or within such longer period as HMRC direct.

[*FA 2014, s 258*].

Duty to provide information about clients

HMRC may give notice to a monitored promoter under which the promoter must give HMRC, for each 'relevant period', the name, address and certain additional prescribed information (see *SI 2015 No 549, Reg 8*) for each client (as defined) for whom such information has not been given for a previous relevant period. Each of the following is a 'relevant period':

(a)   the 'calendar quarter' in which the notice is given (but excluding any time before the monitoring notice takes effect);

(b)   any period from the time the monitoring notice takes effect until the start of the period in (a) above; and

(c)   each subsequent calendar quarter (excluding any time after the monitoring notice ceases to have effect).

A '*calendar quarter*' is a period of three months beginning on 1 January, 1 April, 1 July or 1 October.

Information must be provided within the 30 days beginning with the end of each relevant period or, for a relevant period within (b) above, within the 30 days beginning with the day on which the notice is given, if later.

A similar notice may be given to a person who is an intermediary in relation to a monitored proposal.

Where a promoter or intermediary has provided information under the above provisions in connection with a particular proposal or particular arrangements but an authorised HMRC officer suspects that a person for whom such information has not been provided has been, or is likely to be, a party to transactions implementing the proposal or is a party to a transaction forming the whole or part of the arrangements, the officer may by notice in writing require the promoter or intermediary to provide the information about any such person together with the reason why the information was not provided as required. Information required under a notice must be provided within ten days beginning with the day the notice is given or within such longer period as HMRC direct. A notice does not require information to be provided if it has already been provided under the above provisions.

[*FA 2014, ss 259–261, 283(1); SI 2015 No 549, Regs 8–10*].

Duty to notify HMRC of address

A monitored promoter must inform HMRC of its address within 30 days of the end of any calendar quarter at the end of which the monitoring notice applies. [*FA 2014, s 263*].

Duty of client or intermediary to provide information to promoter

An intermediary or client who is informed of a monitored promoter's reference number must within ten days notify the promoter of his national insurance number and unique taxpayer reference number. If he has neither of those numbers he must inform the promoter of that fact within ten days. There is no need to provide the information if the client or intermediary has previously provided it to the promoter. [*FA 2014, s 265*].

Information powers: further provisions

Failure to provide information

[20.12] Where a person has provided information or produced a document in purported compliance with any of the information powers at **20.9** or **20.11** above (other than those under FA 2014, s 263 or s 265), HMRC may apply to the Tribunal for an order for the person to provide further specified information or produce further specified documents which they have reasonable grounds for suspecting are required by the information power in question or will support or explain information required by the power.

If the Tribunal grants such an order the information or documents must be provided or produced within ten days or such later date as HMRC direct. The duty to provide information or produce a document under such a notice is treated as part of the duty under the original information power (for the purposes of penalties etc.).

[*FA 2014, s 264*].

Appeals

A person given a notice under any of the information powers at **20.9** or **20.11** above (other than those under *FA 2014, s 263* or *s 265*) may appeal against the notice as a whole or against any particular requirement in the notice. There is, however, no right of appeal where the information or documents form part of the person's 'statutory records' or where the Tribunal has approved the giving of the notice (see **20.11** above under 'Information and documents').

Notice of appeal must be given in writing to the HMRC officer who gave the notice within the period of 30 days beginning with the date on which the notice was given and must state the grounds of appeal. A decision on an appeal by the Tribunal is final (so that there is no further right of appeal to the Upper Tribunal or Court of Appeal). Where the Tribunal confirms or varies the notice or a requirement in it, the person to whom the notice was given must comply with the notice or requirement within the period specified by the Tribunal. If the Tribunal does not specify such a period, compliance must be within such period as an HMRC officer reasonably specifies in writing.

Subject to the above, the appeal provisions of *TMA 1970, Pt 5* (see **5** APPEALS) apply to an appeal against a notice.

For this purpose, '*statutory records*' are information and documents which a taxpayer is required to keep and preserve under any enactments relating to any of the taxes to which the high-risk promoter provisions apply. Information and documents cease to be statutory records when the period for which they must be kept and preserved ends.

[*FA 2014, s 266*].

Compliance with a notice

HMRC may specify the form and manner in which information must be provided or documents produced. Documents must be produced for inspection either at a place agreed to by the recipient of the notice and an HMRC officer or at a place (other than one used solely as a dwelling) that an HMRC officer reasonably specifies. Copies of documents can be produced unless the notice requires the production of the original document or an HMRC officer in writing subsequently requests the original document. Where a copy is produced, it must be an exact copy of the original document, which must be retained and unaltered (except for the redaction of any privileged information). Where an officer makes a request for the original document, it must be produced within the period and at the time and by the means reasonably requested by the officer.

The production of a document under these provisions does not break any lien (i.e. any right) claimed on it.

[FA 2014, ss 267, 268; SI 2015 No 549, Reg 11].

Restrictions on information powers

The recipient of a notice under any of the information powers at **20.9** or **20.11** above is not required to:

(i) produce a document if it is not in his possession or power;

(ii) provide or produce information that relates to the conduct of a pending tax appeal or any part of a document containing such information;

(iii) provide journalistic material (within *Police and Criminal Evidence Act 1984, s 13*) or information contained in such material;

(iv) subject to the exceptions below, provide or produce 'personal records' (within *Police and Criminal Evidence Act 1984, s 12*); or

(v) produce a document the whole of which originates more than six years before the giving of the notice.

With regard to (iv) above, a notice may require a person to produce documents that are personal records, omitting any personal information (i.e. information whose inclusion in the documents makes them personal records) and to provide any information in personal records that is not personal information. *[FA 2014, ss 269, 270].*

Legal professional privilege

A notice cannot require a person to provide information in respect of which a claim to legal professional privilege (or, in Scotland, a claim to confidentiality of communications) could be maintained in legal proceedings. *[FA 2014, s 271].*

Tax advisers

A notice under **20.11**(3) or (4) above does not require a 'tax adviser' to provide information about, or to produce documents which are his property and which consist of, communications between him and a person in relation to whose tax affairs he has been appointed or between him and any other tax advisor of such a person, the purpose of which is the giving or obtaining of advice about any of those tax affairs. For this purpose, a *'tax adviser'* is a person appointed (directly or by another tax adviser) to give advice about the tax affairs of another person.

This restriction does not apply to any information, or any document containing information, which explains any information or document which the tax adviser has, as tax accountant, assisted any client in preparing for, or delivering to, HMRC. The restriction is not disapplied if the information concerned, or a document containing the information, has already been provided or produced to an HMRC officer. *[FA 2014, s 272].*

Confidentiality

No duty of confidentiality or other restriction on disclosure (however imposed) prevents the voluntary disclosure to HMRC of information or documents about a monitored promoter of monitored proposals or arrangements by a client or intermediary. *[FA 2014, s 273].*

Concealing, destroying or disposing of documents

[20.13] A person must not conceal, destroy or otherwise dispose of, or arrange for the concealment, destruction or disposal of, a document that is subject to a requirement under the information powers in *FA 2014, s 263* (see 20.9 above) or *FA 2014, ss 255, 257* (see **20.11** above). This does not apply if he does so after the document has been produced to HMRC in accordance with the notice, unless an HMRC officer has notified him in writing that the document must continue to be available for inspection (and has not withdrawn the notification). It also does not apply if a copy of the document was produced in compliance with the notice and the destruction, etc. takes place after the end of the period of six months beginning with the day on which the copy was produced unless within that period, an HMRC officer makes a request for the original document.

Similarly, where a person has been informed that a document is, or is likely to be, the subject of such a notice addressed to him, he must not conceal, destroy or otherwise dispose of, or arrange for the concealment, destruction or disposal of, the document. This does not apply if he acts more than six months after he was so informed (or was last so informed).

A person who conceals, destroys or otherwise disposes of, or arranges for the concealment, destruction or disposal of, a document in breach of the above provisions is treated as having failed to comply with the duty to produce the document under the provision in question. If more than one provision is in question the person is treated as only having failed to comply with the duty under *FA 2014, s 248* or, if that section is not in question, with the duty under *FA 2014, s 257*.

[*FA 2014, Sch 35 paras 6, 7*].

Failure to comply with the above provisions may be a criminal offence. See **20.14** below.

Offences and penalties

[20.14] For penalties under the high-risk promoters provisions, see **51.26** PENALTIES.

It is an offence for a person required to produce a document by a notice under *FA 2014, s 255* (see **20.11** above) which has been approved by the Tribunal to conceal, destroy or otherwise dispose of the document or to arrange for its concealment, destruction or disposal. This does not apply if he does so after the document has been produced to HMRC in accordance with the notice, unless an HMRC officer has notified him in writing that the document must continue to be available for inspection (and has not withdrawn the notification). It also does not apply if a copy of the document was produced in compliance with the notice and the destruction, etc. takes place after the end of the period of six months beginning with the day on which the copy was produced unless within that period, an HMRC officer makes a request for the original document.

It is also an offence for a person to conceal, destroy or otherwise dispose of, or to arrange for the concealment, destruction or disposal of, a document after an HMRC officer has informed him in writing that the document is, or is likely to be, the subject of such a notice and approval for giving the notice is to be obtained from the Tribunal. This does not apply if the person so acts more than six months after he was so informed (or was last so informed).

On summary conviction of either of the above offences the offender is liable to a fine. On conviction on indictment the punishment is imprisonment for a maximum of two years and/or a fine.

[FA 2014, ss 278–280].

Partnerships

[20.15] Persons carrying on a business in partnership (within the meaning of *Partnership Act 1890*) are treated as a person for the purposes of the high-risk promoter provisions. A partnership is treated as continuing to be the same partnership (and the same person) regardless of a change in membership, provided that a person who was a member before the change remains a member after the change. Accordingly, a partnership is taken to have done any act which bound the members (restricted, in the case of a limited partnership, to the general partners) and to have failed to comply with any obligation of the firm (within the meaning of *Partnership Act 1890*) which the members failed to comply with. Where, however, a member has done, or failed to do, an act at any time, the partnership is not treated at any later time as having done or failed to do that act if at that later time neither that member nor any other person who was a member at the earlier time is still a member.

A 'partnership' does not include, for the purposes of the high-risk promoter provisions, a body of persons forming a legal person that is distinct from themselves.

Responsibility of partners

A notice under the high-risk promoter provisions given to a partnership has effect at any time in relation to the persons who are members of the partnership at that time (the *'responsible partners'*). This does not, however, affect any liability of a member who has left the partnership for anything that the responsible partners did or failed to do before he left. Anything which must be done by the responsible partners must be done by all of them (but see below regarding 'nominated partners'). References in the provisions to a right of a person (such as a right of appeal) must be interpreted accordingly.

The responsible partners are jointly and severally liable to any penalty under **51.26** PENALTIES and to any interest on such a penalty, but no amounts can be recovered from a person who did not become a responsible partner until after the act or omission which led to the penalty occurred or, in the case of a daily penalty or interest accruing for a particular day, until after the beginning of that day.

A notice given to a partnership by HMRC must be served either on all of the current partners or on a 'representative partner'. For this purpose a *'representative partner'* is a nominated partner or, if there is no nominated partner, a partner designated by an authorised HMRC officer as a representative partner and notified to the partnership as such.

Anything which must be done by the responsible partners can instead be done by a *'nominated partner'*, i.e. a partner nominated by the majority of the partners to act as the partnership's representatives for the purposes of the high-risk promoter provisions. The partnership must notify HMRC of a nomination or its revocation.

Partnership changes

Where the business of a partnership subject to a conduct notice or monitoring notice starts to be carried on by one of the partners but not in partnership (i.e. where the other partners leave the partnership), the notice continues to apply to the continuing partner.

Where a controlling member of a partnership subject to a conduct notice leaves the partnership and carries on a business as a promoter, an authorised HMRC officer may give that person a replacement conduct notice. If the business is conducted by a partnership of which that person is a controlling member the replacement notice may be given to the partnership, but the notice will cease to have effect if that person leaves the partnership. Similar provisions apply to allow the giving of replacement monitoring notices.

Where a partner in a partnership which is subject to a conduct notice or a monitoring notice ceases to carry on the partnership's business but continues to carry on a part (but not the whole) of the business, an authorised HMRC officer may give that partner a replacement conduct notice or, as appropriate, a replacement monitoring notice. If the departing partner carries on the part of the business in partnership, a replacement notice may be given to that partnership, but the notice will cease to have effect if the partner leaves the partnership. These rules apply whether it is one, some or all of the partners in the original partnership who carry on a part of the business.

A replacement conduct notice ceases to have effect on the date on which the original notice would have ceased to have effect and must state that date as its expiry date. Such a notice may not be given after the expiry of the original notice. A replacement conduct or monitoring notice may not be given to a person if a conduct or monitoring notice previously given to that person still has effect.

[*FA 2014, Sch 36 paras 1–3, 7–13, 15–18*].'

21

Double Tax Relief

The reference to HMRC Capital Gains Manual after the contents list is updated to CG14380.

Current agreements

[21.3] The complete text is updated to read as follows.

'A list is given below of the double tax agreements made by the UK which are currently operative. The agreements have effect to the extent, and as from the operative dates, specified therein (SI numbers in round brackets). Additional notes for certain agreements are given after the list, together with details of agreements made but not yet in force.

Albania (2013/3145 — applies in the UK from 1 April 2014 for corporation tax purposes and from 6 April 2014 for capital gains tax purposes), **Antigua and Barbuda** (1947/2865; 1968/1096), **Argentina** (1997/1777), **Armenia** (2011/2722), **Australia** (1968/305; 1980/707; 2003/3199), **Austria** (1970/1947; 1979/117; 1994/768; 2010/2688), **Azerbaijan** (1995/762),

Bahrain (2012/3075), **Bangladesh** (1980/708), **Barbados** (2012/3076), **Belarus** (1995/2706 — see notes below), **Belgium** (1987/2053; 2010/2979), **Belize** (1947/2866; 1968/573; 1973/2097), **Bolivia** (1995/2707), **Bosnia-Herzegovina** (see note below), **Botswana** (2006/1925), **British Virgin Islands** (2009/3013), **Brunei** (1950/1977; 1968/306; 1973/2098; 2013/3146), **Bulgaria** (1987/2054), **Burma** (see Myanmar below),

Canada (1980/709; 1980/1528; 1985/1996; 2003/2619), **Cayman Islands** (2010/2973), **Chile** (2003/3200), **China** (2011/2724; 2013/3142), **Croatia** (see note below), **Cyprus** (1975/425; 1980/1529), **Czech Republic** (see note below),

Denmark (1980/1960; 1991/2877; 1996/3165),

Egypt (1980/1091), **Estonia** (1994/3207), **Ethiopia** (2011/2725),

Falkland Islands (1997/2985), **Faroe Islands** (2007/3469; 1961/579; 1971/717; 1975/2190 until 6 April 1997), **Fiji** (1976/1342), **Finland** (1970/153; 1980/710; 1985/1997; 1991/2878; 1996/3166), **France** (2009/226),

Gambia (1980/1963), **Georgia** (2004/3325; 2010/2972), **Germany** (2010/2975; 1967/25; 1971/874), **Ghana** (1993/1800), **Greece** (1954/142), **Grenada** (1949/361; 1968/1867), **Guernsey** (1952/1215; 1994/3209), **Guyana** (1992/3207),

Hong Kong (2010/2974), **Hungary** (2011/2726),

Iceland (1991/2879), **India** (1981/1120; 1993/1801; 2013/3147), **Indonesia** (1994/769), **Ireland** (1976/2151, 1976/2152; 1995/764; 1998/3151), **Isle of Man** (1955/1205; 1991/2880; 1994/3208; 2009/228), **Israel** (1963/616; 1971/391), **Italy** (1990/2590), **Ivory Coast** (1987/169),

Jamaica (1973/1329), **Japan** (2006/1924), **Jersey** (1952/1216; 1994/3210), **Jordan** (2001/3924),

Kazakhstan (1994/3211; 1998/2567), **Kenya** (1977/1299), **Kiribati** (as per Tuvalu), **Korea, Republic of (South)** (1996/3168), **Kuwait** (1999/2036),

Latvia (1996/3167), **Lesotho** (1997/2986), **Libya** (2010/243), **Liechtenstein** (2012/3077), **Lithuania** (2001/3925; 2002/2847), **Luxembourg** (1968/1100; 1980/567; 1984/364; 2010/237),

Macedonia (2007/2127), Malawi (1956/619; 1964/1401; 1968/1101; 1979/302), Malaysia (1997/2987; 2010/2971), Malta (1995/763), Mauritius (1981/1121; 1987/467; 2003/2620; 2011/2442), Mexico (1994/3212; 2010/2686), Moldova (2008/1795), Mongolia (1996/2598), Montserrat (1947/2869; 1968/576; 2011/1083), Morocco (1991/2881), Myanmar (1952/751),

Namibia (1962/2352; 1962/2788; 1967/1490), Netherlands (2009/227; 1980/1961; 1983/1902; 1990/2152; 2013/3143), New Zealand (1984/365; 2004/1274; 2008/1793), Nigeria (1987/2057), Norway (2013/3144 — applies in the UK from 1 April 2014 for corporation tax purposes and from 6 April 2014 for capital gains tax purposes; 1985/1998; 2000/3247),

Oman (1998/2568; 2010/2687),

Pakistan (1987/2058), Papua New Guinea (1991/2882), Philippines (1978/184), Poland (2006/3323), Portugal (1969/599),

Qatar (2010/241; 2011/1684),

Romania (1977/57), Russia (1994/3213),

Saudi Arabia (2008/1770), St. Christopher (St. Kitts) and Nevis (1947/2872), Serbia and Montenegro (see note below), Sierra Leone (1947/2873; 1968/1104), Singapore (1997/2988; 2010/2685; 2012/3078), Slovak Republic (Slovakia) (see note below), Slovenia (2008/1796), Solomon Islands (1950/748; 1968/574; 1974/1270), South Africa (1969/864; 2002/3138; 2011/2441), Spain (2013/3152), Sri Lanka (1980/713), Sudan (1977/1719), Swaziland (1969/380), Sweden (1984/366), Switzerland (1978/1408; 1982/714; 1994/3215; 2007/3465; 2010/2689),

Taiwan (2002/3137), Thailand (1981/1546), Trinidad and Tobago (1983/1903), Tunisia (1984/133), Turkey (1988/932), Tuvalu (1950/750; 1968/309; 1974/1271),

Uganda (1952/1213; 1993/1802), Ukraine (1993/1803), U.S.A. (1980/568; 2002/2848), USSR (see note below), Uzbekistan (1994/770),

Venezuela (1996/2599), Vietnam (1994/3216),

Yugoslavia (1981/1815 and see note below),

Zambia (1972/1721; 1981/1816), Zimbabwe (1982/1842).

Shipping & Air Transport only—Algeria (Air Transport only) (1984/362), Brazil (1968/572), Cameroon (Air Transport only) (1982/1841), Ethiopia (Air Transport only) (1977/1297 — now replaced by comprehensive agreement above), Hong Kong (Air Transport) (1998/2566), Hong Kong (Shipping Transport) (2000/3248), Iran (Air Transport only) (1960/2419), Jordan (1979/300), Lebanon (1964/278), Saudi Arabia (Air Transport only) (1994/767), Zaire (1977/1298).

Czechoslovakia

The Agreement published as *SI 1991 No 2876* between the UK and Czechoslovakia is treated as remaining in force between the UK and, respectively, the Czech Republic and the Slovak Republic. (HMRC Statement of Practice 5/93).

USSR

The Agreement published as *SI 1986 No 224* (which also continued in force the Air Transport agreement published as *SI 1974 No 1269*) between the UK and the former Soviet Union was to be applied by the UK as if it were still in force between the UK and the former Soviet Republics until such time as new agreements took effect with particular countries. It later came to light that Armenia, Georgia, Kyrgyzstan, Lithuania and Moldova did not consider themselves bound by the UK/USSR convention and were not operating it in relation to UK residents. Accordingly, the UK ceased to apply it to residents of those countries from 1 April 2002 for corporation tax and from 6 April 2002 for income tax and capital gains tax. (The Agreement published as *SI 2001 No 3925* between the UK and Lithuania has effect from those dates.) A similar discovery has subsequently been made in relation to Tajikistan and the agreement ceased to be applied by the UK from 1 April 2014 for corporation tax and from 6 April 2014 for income tax and capital gains tax. The position for other former Republics (Belarus and Turkmenistan) with which new conventions are not yet in force remains as before. (HMRC Statement of Practice 4/01 (replacing SP 3/92) and Revenue Tax Bulletin June 2001 p 864).

Yugoslavia

The Agreement published as *SI 1981 No 1815* between the UK and Yugoslavia is regarded as remaining in force between the UK and, respectively, Bosnia-Herzegovina, Croatia, and Serbia and Montenegro (and, prior to the implementation of new agreements, Slovenia and Macedonia). (HMRC Statements of Practice 3/04, 3/07).

Copies of double tax agreements and other statutory instruments published from 1987 onwards are available on the Stationery Office website at www.h mso.gov.uk/stat.htm.

Agreements not yet in force

The Agreement with Belarus had not yet entered into force in August 2008 and was then considered unlikely to enter into force in the near future. (HMRC Double Taxation Relief Manual DT3300). A comprehensive agreement with Panama was signed on 29 July 2013 (see *SI 2013 No 3149*). A protocol to the agreement with the Isle of Man was agreed on 10 October 2013 (see *SI 2013 No 3148*). A new agreement with Iceland was signed on 17 December 2013 (see *SI 2014 No 1879*) — applies in the UK from 1 April 2015 for corporation tax purposes and from 6 April 2015 for capital gains tax purposes. A protocol to the agreement with Japan was signed on 17 December 2013 (see *SI 2014 No 1881*) and applies in the UK from 1 April 2015 for corporation tax purposes and from 6 April 2015 for capital gains tax purposes. A new agreement with Zambia was signed on 4 February 2014 (see *SI 2014 No 1876*). A protocol to the agreement with Belgium was signed on 14 March 2014 (see *SI 2014 No 1875*). A protocol to the agreement with Germany was signed on 17 March 2014 (see *SI 2014 No 1874*). A comprehensive agreement with Tajikistan was signed on 1 July 2014 (see *SI 2014 No 3275*). A protocol to the agreement with Canada was signed on 21 July 2014 (see *SI 2014 No 3274*). A comprehensive agreement with Croatia was signed on 15 January 2015. A comprehensive agreement with Algeria was signed on 18 February 2015. A comprehensive agreement with Senegal was signed on 26 February 2015.

Representations about new double tax treaties, or suggestions about desirable changes to existing ones, should be made to HM Revenue & Customs CT, International & Stamps Tax Treaty Team, Room 3C/03, 100 Parliament Street, London SW1A 2BQ. Questions about a particular double tax treaty and its effects on an individual's own tax affairs should be addressed to his local tax office.'

22

Employee Share Schemes

Enterprise management incentives

[22.22] A reference to SI 2014 No 2461 is added to the list of statutory references in the last paragraph.

23

Enterprise Investment Scheme

Introduction

[23.1] The following is added at the end.

'Finance Bill 2015 will include provisions amending the list of excluded activities at **23.9** below, so that, for shares issued on or after 6 April 2015, companies (excluding community organisations) whose trade consists wholly or substantially of the subsidised generation of energy from renewable sources where anaerobic digestion or hydroelectric power is involved, or where a company enters into a contract for difference, will not be eligible under the EIS. See www.gov.uk/government/publications/income-tax-and-capital-gains-t ax-change-to-venture-capital-schemes-for-companies-and-community-organis ations-benefitting-from-energy-subsidies.'

24

Entrepreneurs' Relief

Introduction

[24.1] The following is added at the end.

'Finance Bill 2015 changes

'Two changes to entrepreneurs' relief are to be included in the Finance Bill 2015.

The scope of the relief will be extended to deferred gains which come into charge following a chargeable event under either the ENTERPRISE INVESTMENT SCHEME (23) or SOCIAL INVESTMENT RELIEF (64) scheme. The extension applies to gains which have as their source a qualifying business disposal on or after 3 December 2014. If a gain has been deferred more than once, it is the initial gain which must relate to a qualifying business disposal. Where part of a deferred gain has previously accrued without a claim to entrepreneurs' relief being made in respect of it, it is not possible to claim relief under the new provisions when another part of the same gain subsequently accrues. See www.gov.uk/government/publications/capital-gains-tax-allowing-entrepreneu rs-relief-on-deferred-gains.

Gains arising on disposals on or after 3 December 2014 of goodwill to a company to which the person making the disposal is related will not be eligible for entrepreneurs' relief. See www.gov.uk/government/publications/capital-ga ins-tax-denying-entrepreneurs-relief-for-disposals-of-goodwill-to-related-com panies.'

Material disposal of business assets

[24.3] The following is added at the end of the penultimate paragraph of list item (c).

'The meanings of 'officer' and 'employee' were considered in *Hirst v HMRC* FTT, [2014] UKFTT 924 (TC), 2015 STI 135.'

25

Exemptions and Reliefs

Individual Savings Accounts (ISAs)

[25.30] The first four paragraphs are replaced by the following.

'ISAs are available to individuals over 18 (though see below) who are both resident and ordinarily resident in the UK. The accounts can be made up of cash, stocks and shares and, before 6 April 2005, life insurance (see below). For 2015/16, investors can subscribe up to £15,240 to an ISA in the tax year. For 2014/15, the annual limit is £15,000 (but note that, before 1 July 2014, the annual limit was £11,880 of which a maximum of £5,940 could be saved in cash with one provider). For 2013/14 the overall limit is £11,520 and the cash limit is £5,760; for 2012/13 the limits are £11,289 and £5,640; for 2011/12 they are £10,680 and £5,340; for 2010/11, they are £10,200 and £5,100. See further details below. For 2015/16 the annual limit will be

£15,240. Cash ISAs can be opened by 16 and 17-year olds. There is no statutory lock-in, minimum subscription, minimum holding period or lifetime subscription limit. Withdrawals may be made at any time without loss of tax relief but not so as to allow further subscriptions in breach of the annual maximum.

With effect from 6 April 2015 a surviving spouse or civil partner will be granted an additional ISA allowance equivalent to the value of the deceased spouse or partner's ISAs, so that the tax-free status of the savings may be preserved.

Interest and dividends are free of income tax. Gains arising from assets held within an ISA are not chargeable gains for CGT purposes (and losses are not allowable).

With effect from 1 November 2011 a new 'junior ISA' is introduced for children who did not qualify for a child trust fund (see **25.24** above). Subscriptions of up to £4,080 (£4,080 before 6 April 2015; £3,840 before 1 July 2014; £3720 before 6 April 2014; £3,600 before 6 April 2013) can be made in each tax year and can be saved in cash or stocks and shares. For 2015/16 the annual limit will be £4,080. The funds are locked in until the child reaches adulthood.'

31

HMRC — Confidentiality of Information

Organisations to which HMRC may disclose information

[31.2] The text is updated to read as follows.

'HMRC are authorised to disclose information to the following.

(a) **Charity Commissioners for England and Wales.** HMRC are authorised to disclose certain information to the Charity Commissioners regarding bodies which are or have been charities. Similar provisions apply in Scotland as regards disclosure to the Lord Advocate. [*Charities Act 1993, s 10; Law Reform (Miscellaneous Provisions) (Scotland) Act 1990, s 1; SI 2010 No 588*].

(b) **Department of Trade and Industry, Department of Employment or Office for National Statistics.** HMRC are authorised to disclose, for the purposes of statistical surveys, the names and addresses of employers and information concerning the number of persons employed by individual concerns. [*FA 1969, s 58*].

(c) **Tax authorities of other countries.** HMRC are authorised to disclose information concerning individual taxpayers where it is necessary to the administration or enforcement of double taxation agreements and may be required to disclose information to an advisory commission set up under the Arbitration Convention (*90/436/EEC*). [*TIOPA 2010, ss 126–129; ICTA 1988, s 816(1)(2A)–(5); TCGA 1992, s 277(4)*].

Disclosure may also be made to the tax authorities of other member states of the EU which observe similar confidentiality *and use the information only for taxation purposes. [*FA 2003, s 197(1)–(5)*].

The UK may enter into agreements with other countries for mutual assistance in the enforcement of taxes. Such agreements may include provision for the exchange of information foreseeably relevant to the administration, enforcement or recovery of any UK tax or foreign tax. HMRC may disclose information under such agreements only if satisfied that the confidentiality rules applied by the foreign authorities concerned with respect to the information are no less strict than the equivalent UK rules. [*FA 2006, s 173*]. This power has been exercised to enter into the joint Council of Europe/Organisation for Economic Co-operation and Development Convention on Mutual Administrative Assistance in Tax Matters, signed on behalf of the UK on 24 May 2007. [*SI 2007 No 2126; SI 2011 No 1079*]. In addition to tax enforcement agreements included as part of double tax treaties, the UK has also signed tax enforcement agreements with Jersey (see *SI 2013 No 3151*), Guernsey (*SI 2013 No 3154*) and the Marshall Islands (*SI 2013 No 3153*).

In addition to tax information agreements included as part of double tax treaties (see **21.2** DOUBLE TAX RELIEF), the UK has also signed tax information exchange agreements with Bermuda (*SI 2008 No 1789*), the Isle of Man, Guernsey (*SI 2009 No 3011*), Jersey (*SI 2009 No 3012*), the British Virgin Islands (*SI 2009 No 3013; SI 2014 No 1359*), Anguilla (*SI 2010 No 2677; SI 2014 No 1357*), the Turks and Caicos Islands (*SI 2010 No 2679; SI 2014 No 1360*), Liechtenstein (*SI 2010 No 2678*), Gibraltar (*SI 2010 No 2680; SI 2014 No 1356*), the Bahamas (*SI 2010 No 2684*), St Lucia (*SI 2011 No 1076*), St Vincent and the Grenadines (*SI 2011 No 1078*), Antigua and Barbuda (*SI 2011 No 1075*), St Christopher and Nevis (*SI 2011 No 1077*), Belize (*SI 2011 No 1685*), Grenada (*SI 2011 No 1687*), San Marino (*SI 2011 No 1688*), Dominica (*SI 2011 No 1686*), the Netherlands Antilles, Liberia (*SI 2011 No 2434*), Aruba (*SI 2011 No 2435*), Curacao, Sint Maarten and BES Islands (*SI 2011 No 2433*), the Marshall Islands, Brazil, Uruguay (*SI 2014 No 1358*) and Monaco. For agreements in connection with the EU Savings Directive and special withholding tax, see **21.10** DOUBLE TAX RELIEF.

HMRC may also disclose information to the tax authority of Switzerland pursuant to a request under Article 36 of the UK/Switzerland tax collection agreement (see **48.22** OVERSEAS MATTERS). [*FA 2012, Sch 36 para 25*]. See also **50.27** PAYMENT OF TAX.

(d) **Occupational Pensions Board.** HMRC are authorised to disclose information about pension schemes. [*Social Security Act 1973, s 89(2)*].

(e) **Social Security Departments.** HMRC may disclose information obtained in connection with the assessment or collection of income tax but for self-employed persons they may only disclose the fact that a person has commenced or ceased self-employment together with the identity of that person and information relating to earners employed by that person. [*Social Security Administration Act 1992, s 122*].

HMRC may, and *must* if an authorised social security officer so requires, supply to the social security authorities information held for the purposes of tax credit functions and functions relating to child benefit or guardian's allowance for use by those authorities for the purposes of functions relating to social security benefits, child support, tax credits, war pensions or prescribed evaluation or statistical studies. [*Tax Credits Act 1999, Sch 5 para 2; Tax Credits Act 2002, Sch 5 para 4; SI 2002 Nos 1727, 3036*].

Social security authorities are in turn permitted to supply information to HMRC for investigative purposes. [*FA 1997, s 110*].

(f) **Criminal investigations etc.** HMRC may disclose information to organisations such as the police, the National Criminal Intelligence Service and the National Crime Squad, having a legitimate interest in, and capable of carrying out, criminal investigations and/or bringing proceedings for criminal offences and for the purposes of assisting criminal investigations or proceedings in the UK or elsewhere, including whether such investigations or proceedings should be initiated or brought to an end. Disclosures may also be made to the intelligence services for the purposes of facilitating the carrying out of their functions. [*Anti-terrorism, Crime and Security Act 2001, ss 19, 20*].

See also Revenue Press Release 11 February 2002 and related voluntary Code of Practice on the Disclosure of Information.

Also, HMRC can disclose information to the police to assist investigation into suspected murder or treason (*Royal Commission on Standards of Conduct in Public Life 1976, para 93*).

(g) **Non-UK resident entertainers and sportsmen.** In connection with the deduction of sums representing income tax from certain payments to such persons, HMRC may disclose relevant matters to any person who appears to HMRC to have an interest. [*ITA 2007, s 970(2)(3); ICTA 1988, s 558(4)*].

(h) **Local authorities and Health Departments etc.** As regards information held for the purposes of tax credit functions (see Tolley's Income Tax under Social Security) and functions relating to child benefit or guardian's allowance, HMRC may disclose information to a local authority (or authorised delegate) for use in the administration of housing benefit or council tax benefit. Information must also be provided in the opposite direction if the Board so require but only for use for purposes relating to tax credits etc. [*Tax Credits Act 2002, Sch 5 paras 7, 8*].

As regards information held for the above-mentioned purposes, HMRC may disclose information to Health Departments for use for purposes of prescribed functions relating to health, to relevant Government Departments for purposes of prescribed functions relating to employment or training (with provision also for certain information to pass in the opposite direction) and (as regards information held for child benefit and guardian's allowance functions only) to any civil servant or other person for purposes of prescribed functions relating to provision of specified services concerning participation by young persons in education and training. [*Tax Credits Act 2002, Sch 5 paras 5, 6, 9, 10*].

(i) **Financial Conduct Authority and Prudential Regulation Authority.** HMRC may authorise the disclosure of information to the Financial Conduct Authority or the Prudential Regulation Authority (previously the Financial Services Authority) for the purpose of assisting or enabling that regulator to discharge its functions or to the Secretary of State for the purposes of investigations under *Financial Services and Markets Act 2000, s 168*. [*Financial Services and Markets Act 2000, s 350; Financial Services Act 2012, Sch 12 para 20*]. Note that HMRC may only disclose information in this way if it was obtained or is held in the exercise of a function previously vested in the Inland Revenue. [*CRCA 2005, Sch 2 para 18*].

(j) **Proceeds of crime etc.** Before 1 April 2008, HMRC may disclose information to the Director of the Assets Recovery Agency for the purpose of the exercise of his functions. Following the dissolution of the Agency after 31 March 2008, HMRC may, after that date, disclose information to the Director of Public Prosecutions or the Director of the Serious Fraud Office for the purpose of the exercise of their functions under *Proceeds of Crime Act 2002, Pts 5 and 8*. [*Proceeds of Crime Act 2002, s 436; Serious Crime Act 2007, Sch 8 para 132; SI 2003 No 120; SI 2008 No 755*]. HMRC may also disclose information to the Lord Advocate and the Scottish Ministers in connection with the exercise of their functions in Scotland under *Proceeds of Crime Act 2002, Pt 3* and *Pt 5* respectively. [*Proceeds of Crime Act 2002, s 439*].

(k) **Financial Reporting Review Panel.** HMRC may disclose information to the Financial Reporting Review Panel for the purpose of facilitating the taking of steps by it to discover whether there are grounds for an application to the courts for a declaration that the annual accounts of a company do not comply with *Companies Acts* requirements or determining whether or not to make such an application. HMRC and the Financial Reporting Review Panel have entered into a memorandum of understanding governing the disclosure of information under these provisions. See HMRC Internet Statement, 28 June 2005 and 2005 STI 1197.

(l) **Serious Organised Crime Agency.** HMRC may disclose information to the Serious Organised Crime Agency for the purpose of the exercise of the Agency's functions. [*Serious Organised Crime and Police Act 2005, s 34; SI 2006 No 378*].

(m) **Certification of British films.** In relation to films commencing principal photography on or after 1 January 2007, HMRC may disclose information to the Secretary of State for the purposes of his functions under *Films Act 1985, Sch 1* (certification of films as British films for the purposes of film tax relief). Information so disclosed may be disclosed to the UK Film Council. [*CTA 2009, s 1206; FA 2006, Sch 5 para 24*].

(n) **Criminal Assets Bureau in Ireland.** From 15 February 2008, HMRC may disclose information to the Criminal Assets Bureau ('CAB') in Ireland for the purpose of enabling or assisting the CAB to exercise any of its functions in connection with the proceeds of crime. [*Serious Crime Act 2007, s 85*].

(o) **Prosecuting authorities.** HMRC are permitted to disclose information to the Director of Public Prosecutions (previously the Revenue and Customs Prosecutions Office) for the purpose of enabling the Director to consider whether to institute criminal proceedings in respect of a matter considered in the course of an investigation by HMRC or to give advice in connection with a criminal investigation. In relation to Scotland, HMRC are similarly authorised to disclose information to the Lord Advocate or a procurator fiscal. In Northern Ireland disclosures to the Director of Public Prosecutions for Northern Ireland are likewise permitted. [*CRCA 2005, s 21; SI 2014 No 834*].'

Publication of details of tax agents engaging in dishonest conduct

[31.4] The text is updated to read as follows.

'With effect from 1 April 2013, the Commissioners for HMRC can publish certain information about any individual who incurs a penalty under *FA 2012, Sch 38 para 26* (penalty for dishonest conduct — see **51.21** PENALTIES) if the penalty is more than £5,000.

The Commissioners can publish the individual's name (including previous name or pseudonym), trading name, address, the nature of any business carried on, the amount of the penalty, the periods or times to which the dishonest conduct relates, any other information which they consider appropriate in order to make the individual's identity clear, and the link (if any) between the dishonest conduct and any inaccuracy, failure or action as a result of which information is published under the provisions at **31.3** above. The information can only be first published in the period of one year beginning with the last day on which the penalty becomes final. It cannot continue to be published for more than one year.

Before publishing the information the Commissioners must inform the taxpayer that they are doing so and provide a reasonable opportunity to make representations about whether it should be published.

[*FA 2012, Sch 38 para 28; SI 2013 No 279*].'

32

HMRC Explanatory Publications

HMRC explanatory pamphlets

[32.1] The table of pamphlets is updated.

SA/BK4   Self-Assessment — A General Guide to Keeping Records (June 2003).

SA/BK8	Self-Assessment — Your Guide (June 2004).
CTSA/ BK4	A General Guide to Corporation Tax Self-Assessment (October 2000).
COP 1	Putting things right when we make mistakes (June 2003).
COP 8	Specialist investigations (fraud and bespoke avoidance) (August 2014)
COP 9 (2014)	HMRC investigations where we suspect tax fraud (June 2014).
AO 1	The adjudicator's office for complaints about HMRC and Valuation Office Agency (August 2008)
C/FS	Complaints and putting things right (August 2014)
CC/FS1a	General information about compliance checks (November 2014)
CC/FS1b	General information about checks by compliance centres (September 2012)
CC/FS1c	General information about compliance checks into large businesses (September 2012)
CC/FS2	Compliance checks — requests for information and documents (March 2009)
CC/FS3	Compliance checks — visits — pre-arranged (March 2009)
CC/FS4	Compliance checks — visits — unannounced (March 2009)
CC/FS5	Compliance checks — visits — unannounced — tribunal approved (March 2009)
CC/FS6	Compliance checks — what happens when we find something wrong (March 2009)
CC/FS7a	Compliance checks series — penalties for inaccuracies in returns or documents (September 2012)
CC/FS7b	Compliance checks series — penalties for not telling us about an under-assessment (September 2012)
CC/FS9	Compliance checks — Human Rights Act (April 2009)
CC/FS10	Compliance checks — Suspending penalties for careless errors (August 2009)
CC/FS11	Compliance checks — Penalties for failure to notify (April 2010)
CC/FS13	Compliance checks — Publishing details of deliberate defaulters (April 2010)
CC/FS14	Compliance checks — Managing serious defaulters (November 2014)
CC/FS15	Compliance checks — Self assessment and old penalty rules (February 2011)
CC/FS17	Compliance checks — Higher penalties for income tax and CGT involving offshore matters (May 2012)
CC/FS18(a)	Compliance checks — Late filing penalties for income tax and capital gains tax (May 2012)
CC/FS24	Tax avoidance schemes — accelerated payments (August 2014)
	Take care to avoid a penalty (July 2008)

HMRC 1	HMRC decisions — what to do if you disagree
Pride 1	Taxes and benefits — Information for our lesbian, gay, bisexual and transgender customers (download only — June 2009)
RDR1	Residence, Domicile and the Remittance Basis (October 2013)
TH/FS1	Keeping records for business — what you need to know (February 2011)

34

HMRC Investigatory Powers

HMRC practice in cases of serious tax fraud

[34.13] The text is updated to read as follows.

'The policy of the Commissioners for HMRC in cases of suspected tax fraud, as set out in Code of Practice COP 9, is as follows:

- The Commissioners reserve complete discretion to pursue a criminal investigation with a view to prosecution where they consider it necessary and appropriate.
- Where a criminal investigation is not commenced the Commissioners may decide to investigate using the COP 9 procedure.
- The recipient of COP 9 will be given the opportunity to make a complete and accurate disclosure of all his deliberate and non-deliberate conduct that has led to irregularities in his tax affairs.
- Where HMRC suspect that the recipient has failed to make a full disclosure of all irregularities, the Commissioners reserve the right to commence a criminal investigation with a view to prosecution.
- The term 'deliberate conduct' means that the recipient knew that an entry or entries included in a tax return and/or accounts were wrong but submitted it/them anyway, or that the recipient knew that a tax liability existed but chose not to tell HMRC at the right time.
- In the course of the COP 9 investigation, if the recipient makes materially false or misleading statements, or provides materially false documents, the Commissioners reserve the right to commence a criminal investigation into that conduct as a separate criminal offence.

If the Commissioners decide to investigate using the COP 9 procedure the taxpayer will be given a copy of the above statement by an authorised officer.

Under its published Criminal Investigation Policy (see www.hmrc.gov.uk/pro secutions/crim-inv-policy.htm), HMRC reserve complete discretion to conduct a criminal investigation in any case, with a view to prosecution by the Crown Prosecution Service ('CPS') in England and Wales or the appropriate prosecuting authority in Scotland and Northern Ireland. Examples of the kind of circumstances in which HMRC will generally consider commencing a criminal, rather than civil, investigation are, inter alia, cases involving organised or systematic fraud including conspiracy; cases where an individual holds a position of trust or responsibility; cases where materially false statements are made or materially false documents are provided in the course of a civil investigation; cases where deliberate concealment, deception, conspiracy or corruption is suspected; cases involving the use of false or forged documents; cases involving money laundering; cases where there is a link to suspected wider criminality; and repeated offences.

See *R v CIR (ex p Mead and Cook)* QB 1992, 65 TC 1 as regards HMRC discretion to seek monetary settlements or institute criminal proceedings. See *R v CIR (ex p Allen)* QB 1997, 69 TC 442 for an unsuccessful application for judicial review of a Revenue decision to take criminal proceedings. HMRC have an unrestricted power to conduct a prosecution in the Crown Court, there being no requirement for the consent of the Attorney-General (*R (oao Hunt) v Criminal Cases Review Commission* DC, [2000] STC 1110). See also **30.2** HMRC — ADMINISTRATION.

The Crown Prosecution Service is not precluded from instituting criminal proceedings in circumstances where the Revenue has accepted a monetary settlement (*R v W and another* CA, [1998] STC 550). However, the Revenue in commenting on this case stated that the CPS will ordinarily bring proceedings that encompass tax evasion charges only where that evasion is incidental to allegations of non-fiscal criminal conduct (Revenue Tax Bulletin June 1998 pp 544, 545).

Statements made or documents produced by or on behalf of a taxpayer are admissible as evidence in proceedings against him notwithstanding that reliance on HMRC's practice above or on their policy for mitigating penalties (see **51.29** PENALTIES) may have induced him to make or produce them. [*TMA 1970, s 105*].

See generally HMRC Fraud Civil Investigation Manual.

The fraudulent evasion of *income tax* (not capital gains tax) on behalf of oneself or another person is itself a criminal offence. [*TMA 1970, s 106A; FA 2000, s 144; TIOPA 2010, Sch 7 para 95*].

Contractual disclosure facility

The contractual disclosure facility (CDF) commenced on 31 January 2012 is an opportunity offered to taxpayers to tell HMRC about any tax fraud in which they have been involved. See www.hmrc.gov.uk/admittingfraud/ownin gup.htm. HMRC write to taxpayers whom they suspect have committed a tax fraud; their letter will offer a CDF contract and will be accompanied by a copy of COP 9 (see above). Taxpayers have 60 days from date of receipt to either accept or formally reject the offer of a contract. If they accept, they must produce an Outline Disclosure within the same 60-day period; this should contain a brief description of the frauds committed, a formal admission of deliberately bringing about a loss of tax, details of any non-fraudulent irregularities and any proposals for a payment on account. If the Outline Disclosure is accepted, the taxpayer will be required to make progress towards the production of a Certificate of Full Disclosure.

Under the terms of the CDF contract the taxpayer will not be criminally investigated, with a view to prosecution, for matters covered by the Outline Disclosure. The customer's co-operation will have the potential to maximise reductions in penalties. If the taxpayer rejects the offer of a contract or makes no response, HMRC have the option of starting a criminal investigation, though in most cases they will pursue a civil investigation.

See also HMRC Fraud Civil Investigation Manual FCIM101000 where the CDF contract is offered before 30 June 2014 and FCIM200000 where it is offered on or after that date.

If a taxpayer wishes to own up to a fraud without waiting to be contacted by HMRC, he may complete form CDF1 (www.hmrc.gov.uk/admittingfraud/cdf 1.pdf); HMRC will then consider the taxpayer for a CDF contract.

Simon's Taxes. See **A6.1007–1014.**'

37

Incorporation and Disincorporation Reliefs

Transfer of business to a company — incorporation relief

[37.2] The following is added at the end of the fifth paragraph.

'See also *Roelich v HMRC* FTT, [2014] UKFTT 579 (TC); 2014 STI 2891.'

The reference to HMRC Capital Gains Manual in the paragraph before the heading 'Interaction with other reliefs' is updated to CG65700–65765.

38

Indexation

Calculation of indexation allowance

[38.2] The final table of retail prices index factors is updated to read as follows.

	2012	2013	2014
Jan	238.0	245.8	252.6
Feb	239.9	247.6	254.2
Mar	240.8	248.7	254.8
Apr	242.5	249.5	255.7
May	242.4	250.0	255.9
Jun	241.8	249.7	256.3
Jul	242.1	249.7	256.0

	2012	2013	2014
Aug	243.0	251.0	257.0
Sep	244.2	251.9	257.6
Oct	245.6	251.9	257.7
Nov	245.6	252.1	257.1
Dec	246.8	253.4	257.5

41

Late Payment Interest and Penalties

Late payment penalty

[41.10] The first paragraph is updated as follows.

'A new unified penalty code for failure to make payments on time (the '*late payment penalty*') has been introduced across a range of taxes including capital gains tax and corporation tax. The code applies for capital gains tax purposes with effect from 6 April 2011 to tax payable for 2010/11 and subsequent years. It is expected that the code will apply from 2015 for corporation tax purposes. The code does, however, already apply to corporation tax due under an exit charge payment plan, with effect where the first day after the period of nine months beginning immediately after the accounting period in question falls on or after 11 December 2012. The penalty code is described below, but only to the extent that it relates to capital gains tax and corporation tax. For capital gains tax (and income tax) purposes, the late payment penalty replaces surcharges on unpaid tax (see **41.6** above).'

43

Losses

Assets of negligible value

[43.11] The following paragraph is added after the seventh paragraph.

'In *Drown & Leadley (JJ Leadley's Executors) v HMRC* FTT, [2014] UKFTT 892 (TC); 2014 STI 3707, an individual (L) subscribed for shares in two companies which subsequently became insolvent. In May 2010 L was killed in a motoring accident. His executors submitted claims for relief under *ITA 2007, s 131* (see **43.15** below) on the basis that the shares had become of negligible value by the date of L's death. HMRC accepted that the shares had become of negligible value but rejected the claims on the basis that any claim had to be made by the shareholder and could not be made posthumously by a shareholder's executors. The First-tier Tribunal allowed the executors' appeals, holding that 'there is nothing any of the relevant Acts that expressly provides that personal representatives can, or cannot, make claims in respect of the deceased's chargeability which the deceased could have made had he lived to file his return'. Applying a purposive interpretation of *s 131* and *s 24*, 'the personal representatives of the deceased are treated as the deceased in so far as they are returning the deceased's own tax liability'.'

44

Market Value

Quoted shares and securities

[44.3] The text is replaced by the following.

'The market value of quoted shares and securities is determined as follows.

6 April 2015 onwards

The market value of shares, securities or strips which are included in the official UK list is:

*   on any day the Stock Exchange is open, the lower of the two prices quoted in the Stock Exchange Daily Official List as the closing price for that day plus one-half of the difference between those prices; and
*   on any day the Stock Exchange is closed, that value on the latest previous day on which it was open.

The above method of valuation does not apply for computing the value of shares or securities where special circumstances may affect the value.

The market value of securities or strips which are not included in the official UK list but are listed on a recognised foreign stock exchange is:

*   on any day the exchange is open, the closing price shown in the exchange list for that day or, if more than one price is shown, the lower of the two prices plus one-half of the difference between them; and
*   on any day the exchange is closed, that value on the latest previous day on which it was open.

If securities are quoted in more than one foreign exchange list, then any foreign exchange list published for a foreign exchange which is regarded as the major exchange for such securities is to be used to determine the market value. If there is no such exchange, any foreign exchange list for an exchange in the territory in which the issuing company is resident is used in preference to any other such list. If a strip or a security exchanged for strips of that security is quoted in more than one foreign exchange list, any such list published for a foreign stock exchange in the territory of the issuing government is used in preference to any other such list and any such list published for a major exchange in that territory for such strips or securities is used in preference to any other such list.

[*TCGA 1992, s 272(3)(4); SI 2015 Nos 616, 635*].

Before 6 April 2015

Before 6 April 2015, the market value of shares and securities quoted in The Stock Exchange Daily Official List is the lesser of:

(a)   the lower of the two prices quoted in The Stock Exchange Daily Official List for the relevant date, plus a quarter of the difference between those prices (*'the quarter-up rule'*); and

(b)   the average of the highest and lowest prices for normal bargains recorded on that date, if any.

If the London trading floor is closed on the relevant date, the prices are to be taken by reference to the latest previous date or to the earliest subsequent date, whichever produces the lower figure.

The above method of valuation does not apply for computing the value of shares as at 6 April 1965 (see **8.2** ASSETS HELD ON 6 APRIL **1965**), nor where special circumstances may affect the value.

[TCGA 1992, s 272(3)(4)(6), Sch 11 para 6(1)(2)(4), para 7(1)].

See *Hinchcliffe v Crabtree* HL 1971, 47 TC 419.

Units in unit trusts

Units in unit trusts, subject to similar valuation rules at 6 April 1965 (as above), are valued at the lower of the two prices published by the managers on the relevant date or if no price is published at that time, on the latest date before the relevant date. *[TCGA 1992, s 272(5)(6), Sch 11 para 6(1)(3)]*.

Simon's Taxes. See C2.122.'

Unquoted shares

[44.4] A reference to *Green v HMRC* FTT, [2014] UKFTT 396(TC); 2014 STI 2235 is added at the end of the penultimate paragraph.

48

Overseas Matters

UK resident participator in overseas resident company

[48.7] The following is added to the end of the first paragraph.

'The ECJ has held that the provisions contravene EU law — see *European Commission v United Kingdom* ECJ (C-112/14), [2015] STC 591.'

50

Payment of Tax

Introduction

[50.1] The final paragraph is amended to read as follows.

'Provisions are to be introduced in a 2015 Finance Bill to empower HMRC to recover tax debts of £1,000 or more directly from the bank accounts of taxpayers who have the financial ability to pay and who have been contacted multiple times by HMRC in respect of outstanding debts. See HMRC Guidance Note 25 November 2014 at www.gov.uk/government/publications/i ssue-briefing-direct-recovery-of-debts and www.gov.uk/government/publicatio ns/direct-recovery-of-debts-due-to-hmrc-from-debtors-bank-and-building-soci ety-accounts.'

Corporation tax (on chargeable gains)

The section headed 'Quarterly accounting by large companies' is replaced by the following.

' 'Large' companies pay corporation tax under a system of *quarterly accounting* (i.e. payment by instalments). [*TMA 1970, s 59E; FA 2012, Sch 20 para 12*].

'Large' companies are those with profits (including UK dividend income, other than intra-group dividends, plus tax credits) exceeding £1,500,000 in an accounting period, divided by one plus the number of related 51% group companies (within *CTA 2010, s 279F*) if any. For accounting periods beginning before 1 April 2015, the £1,500,000 limit is divided by one plus the number of active associated companies if any. However, such a company is not treated as 'large' in respect of an accounting period if its total corporation tax liability for that period does not exceed £10,000, which might be the case if it would otherwise be large only by reference to the number of its related 51% group companies or associated companies or the level of its dividend income. A company is also exempt from payment by instalments for an accounting period if it was not 'large' in the 12 months preceding the accounting period and its profits for the accounting period do not exceed £10 million, divided by one plus the number of related 51% group companies (or, for accounting periods beginning before 1 April 2015, active associated companies) as at the end of the preceding accounting period. Each of these monetary limits is proportionately reduced for accounting periods of less than 12 months.

The first instalment is due 6 months and 14 days into the accounting period and the last is due 3 months and 14 days after the end of the accounting period. Interim instalments are due at quarterly intervals. Except for accounting periods of less than 12 months, the amount of each instalment should be one quarter of the total liability (or, under the transitional provisions below, the total payable by instalments). Interest on tax underpaid by any instalment will run from the due date of that instalment. In cases of deliberate or reckless non-payment or underpayment, a penalty of up to twice the amount of interest may be charged. Subject to similar penalty for fraud or negligence, a company may claim repayment of tax paid by instalments if its circumstances change such that the total liability is likely to be less than previously calculated.

See Revenue Tax Bulletins February 2000 pp 723–726 and April 2001 pp 831–836 for practical articles on the operation of the system. HMRC are given extensive powers to require information and records to ascertain reasons for non-payment of an instalment, the validity of a repayment claim or whether the amount of an instalment is consistent with the quality and quantity of information available as to the company's likely corporation tax liability. See below re HMRC guidance on use of their information and penalty powers.

[*SI 1998 No 3175; SI 2014 No 2409*].

HMRC have published guidance outlining the way in which they will use their information and penalty powers under the above regulations; the information powers are not intended for routine use, and the majority of cases of late or inadequate payment will attract only an interest charge, not a penalty. A penalty will be sought in only the most serious cases involving flagrant abuse of the regulations. (Revenue Press Release 8 June 1999). Further guidance on 'acceptable' methods of estimating quarterly instalments has been published on HMRC's website (Revenue Internet Statement 28 June 2002).

Penalties are also chargeable for non-compliance with a notice to produce information, records etc. [*TMA 1970, s 98*].'

Collection and enforcement

[50.18] The section headed 'Recovery of debts through the PAYE system' is replaced by the following text.

'For 2012/13 onwards, HMRC has the power to collect tax debts, including capital gains tax, through the PAYE system (where the taxpayer is an employee) by making adjustments to the taxpayer's tax code. For 2014/15 and earlier years, deductions of more than £3,000 in a single tax year require the consent of the taxpayer.

For 2015/16 onwards, the £3,000 limit is increased for unpaid self-assessment debts of taxpayers with a primary source of annual PAYE income of £30,000 or over. A graduated scale applies so that a maximum of £17,000 can be coded out for a person with earnings over £90,000. The £3,000 limit continues to apply to self-assessment balancing payments.

[*ITEPA 2003, s 684; SI 2003 No 2682, Reg 14A; SI 2011 Nos 1583, 1584, 1585; SI 2014 Nos 2438, 2689*].

See Tolley's Income Tax for full coverage of PAYE.'

51

Penalties

Introduction

[51.1] the following paragraph is added at the end.

'Legislation will be included in the Finance Bill 2015 to strengthen the penalties for offshore non-compliance. From a date to be specified in a Treasury Order but expected to be 1 April 2016 the offshore penalty regime will be extended to cover cases where the proceeds of domestic non-compliance are situated or held outside of the UK, and to have four levels of penalty instead of three. From the date of Royal Assent to the Finance Act 2015, the regime will include a new type of penalty which is triggered following a movement of offshore assets to continue evading tax (an offshore transfer). See www.gov.uk/government/publications/strengthening-penalties-for-offshore-non-compliance.'

52

Private Residences

Introduction

[52.1] The following is added at the end.

'**Charge to CGT on disposals of residential property by non-UK residents**

The scope of capital gains tax is to be extended to include disposals by non-UK residents of UK residential property interests. The charge will apply to individuals and to certain companies. Some changes are also being made to private residence relief. The legislation will be included in Finance Bill 2015 and the new charge will apply to disposals made on or after 6 April 2015.

The main approach for calculating the gain will be to rebase the property to its market value at 6 April 2015 so that only the gain realised over that value (after deduction of any allowable costs incurred after then) is subject to the charge. Alternatively, provided the disposal is not also subject to ATED-related capital gains tax (see **14.10** COMPANIES), the taxpayer can make an irrevocable election to either time apportion the whole gain over the period of ownership, or to compute the gain over the whole period of ownership. The resulting gains are apportioned to reflect the number of days when the asset is used as a dwelling. Non-resident companies will benefit from indexation. To the extent that a gain is ATED-related then ATED-related capital gains tax will continue to apply at 28%. The remaining part of the gain post–6 April 2015 will be subject to the extended CGT charge on non-residents. Losses on disposals of UK residential property will generally be ring-fenced for use against gains on such properties arising to the same non-UK resident person, but unused losses accrued when non-UK resident will be general allowable losses for use against chargeable gains when UK-resident. The rules for private residence relief are also changing in relation to disposals on or after 6 April 2015. A dwelling house will not be treated as occupied as a residence for the purposes of private residence relief in a tax year or partial tax year during the period of ownership in which the individual was not resident in the territory in which the dwelling house is situated, unless in a full tax year he (or his spouse or civil partner) spends at least 90 days in the dwelling, and in a partial tax year he spends at least the appropriate proportion of 90 days there. For these purposes an individual is resident in an overseas territory if he is liable to tax in that territory by reason of his domicile or residence, unless he is only liable on income from sources in that territory or capital situated there.

See HMRC Guidance Note 28 November 2014, 'Responses to consultation on non-residents' CGT charge' and www.gov.uk/government/publications/capital-gains-tax-non-residents-and-uk-property.'

Exemption generally

[52.2] The following is added at the end of the paragraph before the heading 'Spouses and civil partners'.

'In *Ive and another v HMRC* FTT, [2014] UKFTT 436 (TC); 2014 STI 2523, a couple's occupation of a flat for 25 days was held not to amount to residence.'

Election for main residence

[52.9] The following is added at the end of the first paragraph.

'The Government was considering removing the ability for a person to make a main residence election in order to facilitate the introduction of a charge to CGT for non-residents on disposals of residential property for 2015/16 onwards. However, following consultation this proposal has been withdrawn (and see instead the proposals at **52.1** above). See HMRC Guidance Note 28 November 2014, 'Responses to consultation on non-residents' CGT charge'.'

53

Qualifying Corporate Bonds

Definitions

[53.3] The following is added to the end of list item (b).

'In *Trigg v HMRC* FTT 2014, [2015] SFTD 142, bonds which were denominated in sterling but which had been issued with a provision for their conversion into euros if the UK were to adopt the euro were held not to be prevented from being qualifying corporate bonds as a result of the provision.'

Reorganisation of share capital

[53.4] The following paragraph is added immediately before the heading 'Miscellaneous'.

'In *Hancock v HMRC* FTT, [2014] SFTD 1163, a married couple held the entire share capital of a company (B). In 2000 they sold the shares to another company (L), receiving loan notes as consideration. The terms of issue of the loan notes included a provision enabling the noteholders to require repayment in US dollars, which prevented the loan notes from constituting qualifying corporate bonds within *TCGA 1992, s 117*. The sale agreement also included provision for further consideration depending on the subsequent performance of B's business. In 2001 the couple received further loan notes under this provision. These further notes initially also included a provision enabling the noteholders to require repayment in US dollars, but that provision was removed by deeds of variation in 2002, with the result that these further notes did constitute qualifying corporate bonds. In May 2003 the couple exchanged both their QCB and non-QCB holdings of loan notes for further loan notes, which constituted qualifying corporate bonds, and which were redeemed in June 2003. HMRC issued assessments charging CGT under *TCGA 1992, s 116*. The couple appealed, contending that *s 116* did not apply where a holding which consisted partly but not wholly of qualifying corporate bonds was exchanged for a holding of qualifying corporate bonds, as was the case with regard to their exchange of loan notes in May 2003, so that their gain on the loan notes which had not been qualifying corporate bonds was rolled over into the notes which they had acquired in May 2003; and that their redemption of the loan notes in June 2003 was exempt from CGT under *TCGA 1992, s 115(1)*, since those notes were qualifying corporate bonds. The First-tier Tribunal accepted these contentions and allowed their appeal, observing that 'there appears to be an unfortunate mismatch between the introductory provisions of *s 116(1)(b)* on the one hand, and the definitional provisions of *s 116(3)* and *(4)* which feed into the operative provisions'. *TCGA 1992, s 116(1)* appeared to envisage 'a situation where either the original shares or the new holding would not consist entirely of a QCB, but would include both a QCB and a non-QCB'. He held that although 'Parliament cannot have intended to allow the non-QCB element of a conversion of securities into QCBs to escape taxation', that was 'the effect of the clear words of *s 116(1)(b)*'.'

54

Remittance Basis

Chargeable gains remitted to the UK

[54.3] The paragraph following the (a)–(c) list is amended to read as follows.

'In (a)(iii), (b)(iii) and (c)(iii) above, 'in respect of a relevant debt' would appear to mean 'to satisfy, or partly satisfy, a relevant debt'. In addition, if property (including income or gains) is used to pay interest on a debt, it is regarded as used in respect of the debt. HMRC consider that foreign income and gains used as collateral for a loan are used in respect of the relevant debt, so there is a taxable remittance when the loan is brought to the UK. Where foreign income and gains are also used to pay interest on the debt or to repay the borrowed capital the income or gains are also used in respect of a relevant debt and are treated as a remittance. In such circumstances there are potentially two possible sources of a taxable remittance. Before 4 August 2014 HMRC operated a concession under which collateral in commercial situations was not treated as a remittance if regular servicing payments were made, but this concession has been withdrawn. Where a taxpayer who used foreign income or gains as collateral for a loan before 4 August 2014, HMRC will take no action to assess those remittances if the loan arrangements were within the terms of the concession if either the taxpayer gives a written undertaking (which is subsequently honoured) by 31 December 2015 that the foreign income or gains security either has been, or will be replaced by non-foreign income or gains security before 5 April 2016, or the loan or part of the loan that was remitted to the UK either has been, or will be repaid before 5 April 2016. See HMRC Residence, Domicile and Remittance Basis Manual RDRM33170 and HMRC Notice 4 August 2014.'

Charge of £30,000 or £50,000 for claiming the remittance basis

[54.5] The third paragraph is updated to read as follows.

'For the years 2008/09 to 2011/12 inclusive, only the seven-year test existed and the charge could not exceed £30,000. For 2012/13 onwards, the seven-year test and £30,000 charge do continue, but if the individual meets the twelve-year test the charge is increased to £50,000. The twelve-year test must therefore be applied first. For 2015/16 onwards, the £50,000 charge will increase to £60,000 and a new charge of £90,000 will be introduced for individuals who have been UK resident in at least 17 of the last 20 tax years. See www.gov.uk/government/publications/increase-to-remittance-basis-charge .'

59

Seed Enterprise Investment Scheme

Introduction

[59.1] The following is added at the end.

'Finance Bill 2015 will include provisions amending the meaning of 'qualifying trade' (by amending the list of 'excluded activities' at **23.9** ENTERPRISE INVESTMENT SCHEME — see **59.31** below), so that, for shares issued on or after 6 April 2015, companies (excluding community organisations) whose trade consists wholly or substantially of the subsidised generation of energy from renewable sources where anaerobic digestion or hydroelectric power is involved, or where a company enters into a contract for difference, will not be eligible under the

SEIS. See www.gov.uk/government/publications/income-tax-and-capital-gains
-tax-change-to-venture-capital-schemes-for-companies-and-community-organ
isations-benefitting-from-energy-subsidies.'

62

Shares and Securities

Scheme of reconstruction involving issue of securities

[62.7] The reference to HMRC Capital Gains Manual immediately before the
heading 'Anti-avoidance' is updated to CG52720–52728.

63

Shares and Securities — Identification Rules

Capital gains tax — identification rules on or after 6 April 2008

[63.2] The first five paragraphs are updated to read as follows.

'See **63.1** above for **a summary** of the capital gains tax identification rules for
disposals on or after 6 April 2008 as detailed below. **The provisions described
below do not apply for the purposes of corporation tax on chargeable gains.**

The identification rules detailed below apply to disposals on or after 6 April
2008 for the purposes of capital gains tax. They apply for the purpose of
identifying a disposal of shares with an acquisition of shares etc. of the same
class made by the person making the disposal and held by him in the same
capacity as that in which he makes the disposal. For identification purposes,
disposals are considered in the date order in which they take place. These
rules override any identification purporting to be made by the disposal itself or
by a transfer or delivery giving effect to it.

Shares etc. held by a person who acquired them as an employee of the
company concerned or of anyone else and on terms which for the time being
restrict his right to dispose of them (known as 'clogged shares') are treated as
being of a different class from both:

* shares etc. held by him in the same company and acquired otherwise
  than as an employee; and
* shares etc. held by him in the same company which are not, or are no
  longer, subject to the same restrictions.

Upon the removal of restrictions, where the clogged shares form a separate
section 104 holding (see below) that holding is merged with any such holding
for shares of the same class in the same company which are not clogged.
(HMRC Capital Gains Manual CG51580).'

'Section 104 holdings' of securities

[63.4] The section headed 'Effect of pooling' is updated to read as follows.

'Effect of pooling

Any securities of the same class to which pooling applied and held by the same person in the same capacity immediately before the '1985 date' (see 63.3 above) are pooled as a single asset which grows or diminishes as acquisitions and disposals are made on or after that date. Securities of the same class acquired for the first time on or after the '1985 date' are pooled as a single asset in the same way. This treatment has no effect on any market value that has to be ascertained.

Shares and securities of a company are not to be treated as being of the same class unless they are so treated by the practice of the Stock Exchange or would be so treated if dealt with on the Stock Exchange.

The single asset is referred to as the 'section 104 holding') and the part disposal rules apply on any disposal other than one of the whole holding.

A separate 'section 104 holding' applies in relation to any securities held by a person to whom they were issued as an employee of the company or of any other person on terms which restrict his rights to dispose of them, so long as those terms are in force (known as 'clogged shares'). While such a separate 'section 104 holding' exists the owner of it is treated as holding it in a different capacity to that in which he holds any other securities of the same class. Upon the removal of restrictions, two such separate 'section 104 holdings' merge. (HMRC Capital Gains Manual CG51580).'

64

Social Investment Relief

Introduction

[64.1] The following paragraph is added after the fifth paragraph.

'Two changes are to be made to the scheme in the Finance Bill 2015. The changes will apply to investments made on or after a date to be specified once State aid approval has been obtained. The current limit on the amount raised under the scheme at 64.16 below will be replaced by a new annual investment limit of £5 million with an overall limit of £15 million on total investment. The Bill will also make provision for regulations to be made extending the scheme to investments in certain small horticultural and agricultural projects and activities for which a feed in tariff subsidy is receivable. See www.gov.uk/government/publications/income-tax-and-capital-gains-tax-enlarging-the-social-investment-tax-relief-scheme and www.gov.uk/government/publications/income-tax-and-capital-gains-tax-change-to-venture-capital-schemes-for-companies-and-community-organisations-benefitting-from-energy-subsidies.'

Social enterprises

[64.2] The section headed 'Accredited social impact contractors' is updated as follows.

'An *'accredited social impact contractor'* is a company limited by shares that is accredited under these provisions as a social impact contractor. Applications for accreditation must be made to a Minister of the Crown in a form and manner to be specified. A Minister is to accredit a company only if satisfied that (i) it has entered into a 'social impact contract'; (ii) it is established for the sole purpose of entering into and carrying out such a contract; and (iii) its activities in carrying out the contract will not consist wholly, or as to a substantial part, in 'excluded activities' (within **64.27** below). If, subsequently, a Minister is satisfied that condition (ii) or (iii) has ceased to be met in relation to an accredited social impact contractor, he must withdraw the accreditation with effect from the time the condition ceased to be met or a later time.

The accreditation process is administered by the Minister for the Cabinet Office; for guidance see www.gov.uk/government/publications/social-investm ent-tax-relief-accreditation-for-sib-contractors. A company can appeal against a refusal to grant, or the withdrawal of, an accreditation.

A *'social impact contract'* is a contract that meets the following criteria.

(1) A 'contracting authority' within *SI 2006 No 5, Reg 3(1)* (which includes Minsters of the Crown, government departments, the Houses of Parliament, local authorities, fire and police authorities, etc.) must be a party to the contract.

(2) The contract must define the outcomes intended to be achieved.

(3) The Minister for the Cabinet Office must be satisfied that those outcomes have a social or environmental purpose (as defined) and satisfy the conditions specified in Part 2B of the Cabinet Office's guidance (see above).

(4) Where services are to be provided under the contract, the contract must distinguish between those services and the defined outcomes intended to arise from the services.

(5) The defined outcomes must be capable of being objectively measured, and the method of measurement must be set out in the contract.

(6) The contract must provide for the progress towards achieving the defined outcome to be assessed at intervals which the Minister for the Cabinet Office is satisfied are appropriate.

(7) At least 60% of the total payments what could be made by the contracting authority to the company must be conditional on achieving defined outcomes which the Minister for the Cabinet Office is satisfied meet the criteria in (3) and (5) above.

An accreditation as a social impact contractor has effect for a period beginning with the day specified in the accreditation and of a length specified in, or determined in accordance with, the accreditation. The start date may be backdated but cannot be earlier than 6 April 2014. An accredited social impact contractor must notify the Minister of any change in name or address and of any changes to the social impact contract. It must also notify the Minister if any of the conditions or requirements of accreditation cease to be met. An annual report must be made to the Minister.

[*ITA 2007, ss 257JD–257JH; FA 2014, Sch 11 para 1; SI 2014 No 3066*].

Social impact contracts (known as social impact bonds) are expected to be awarded by public sector bodies for the delivery of social outcomes; payment will be made according to outcomes agreed with the contractor and will be dependent on the desired social outcomes being achieved.'

The gross assets requirement

[64.17] The text is updated to read as follows.

'If the social enterprise is a single company, the value of its gross assets must not exceed £15 million immediately before the investment is made and must not exceed £16 million immediately afterwards. If the social enterprise is a parent company, the gross assets test applies by reference to the aggregate gross assets of all the group members (disregarding certain assets held by any group company which correspond to liabilities of another). [*ITA 2007, s 257MC; FA 2014, Sch 11 para 1*]. HMRC SP 2/06 (see **23.5** ENTERPRISE INVESTMENT SCHEME) applies for this purpose.'

68

Underwriters at Lloyd's

Conversion to underwriting through successor company

[68.8] The following is added at the end.

'Conversion of partnership to underwriting through successor company

Provisions similar to those above apply to the conversion of a partnership to underwriting through a successor company where conditions broadly equivalent to those at (a)–(e) above are met. Rollover relief on the disposal of outstanding syndicate capacity is available for such disposals on or after 19 December 2014. Rollover relief on the disposal of assets of the partnership's ancillary trust fund is available for disposals of such assets on or after that date (even if the disposal of syndicate capacity is made before that date). [*FA 1993, s 179B, Sch 20A paras 5A–5D, 9A, 11; SI 2014 No 3133*].'

70

Venture Capital Trusts

Introduction

[70.1] The following new paragraph is added at the end.

'Finance Bill 2015 will include provisions amending the meaning of 'qualifying trade' (by amending the list of 'excluded activities' at **23.9** ENTERPRISE INVEST-MENT SCHEME — see **70.4** below), so that, for shares issued to the VCT on or after 6 April 2015, companies (excluding community organisations) whose trade consists wholly or substantially of the subsidised generation of energy from renewable sources where anaerobic digestion or hydroelectric power is involved, or where a company enters into a contract for difference, will not be a qualifying holding under the scheme. See www.gov.uk/government/publicat ions/income-tax-and-capital-gains-tax-change-to-venture-capital-schemes-for-companies-and-community-organisations-benefitting-from-energy-subsidies.'

Relief in respect of investments

[70.7] The last paragraph before the heading 'Linked sales' is updated as follows.

'An individual or nominee subscribing for eligible shares may obtain from the VCT a certificate giving details of the subscription and certifying that certain conditions for relief are satisfied. [*SI 1995 No 1979, Reg 9; SI 2014 No 1929*].'

Budget Summary 2015

PERSONAL TAXATION	2015/6	2014/15
Personal allowance		
basic	£10,600	£10,000
personal allowance income limit	£100,000	£100,000
born between 6.4.1938 and 5.4.1948	£10,600	£10,500
born before 6.4.1938	£10,660	£10,660
age allowance income limit*	£27,700	£27,000
minimum where income exceeds limit	£10,600	£10,000
transferable allowance	£1,060	N/A
Married couple's allowance (10% relief)		
either partner born before 6.4.1935	£8,355	£8,165
age allowance income limit	£27,700	£27,000
minimum where income exceeds limit	£3,220	£3,140
Blind person's allowance	£2,290	£2,230
Income tax rates		
Starting savings rate**	0%	10%
on income up to	£5,000	£2,880
Basic rate	20%	20%
on taxable income up to	£31,785	£31,865
Higher rate	40%	40%
on taxable income over	£31,785	£31,865
Additional rate	45%	45%
on taxable income over	£150,000	£150,000
Lower rate on dividend income	10%	10%
Higher rate on dividend income	32.5%	32.5%
Additional rate on dividend income	37.5%	37.5%
Pension schemes allowances		
Annual allowance	£40,000	£40,000
Lifetime allowance	£1,250,000	£1,250,000
ISA subscription limits		
Adult ISA	£15,240	£15,000
Junior ISA	£4,080	£4,000

*For 2015/16 the age allowance income limit for personal allowances applies only to those born before 6.4.1938.

**Starting rate applies only to savings income. If taxable non-savings income is above this limit, the starting rate is not applicable.

COMPANY TAXATION	FY2015	FY2014
Corporation tax rates		
All companies (except below)	20%	21%
Companies with small profits	N/A	20%
— 20% rate limit	N/A	£300,000
— marginal relief limit	N/A	£1,500,000
— marginal relief fraction	N/A	1/400
— marginal rate	N/A	21.25%

CAPITAL GAINS TAX	2015/16	2014/15
Rate – standard rate	18%	18%
— higher rate	28%	28%
— trustees and personal representatives	28%	28%
— entrepreneurs' relief rate	10%	10%
Annual exemption - individuals	£11,100	£11,000
— personal representatives	£11,100	£11,000
— trustees	£5,550*	£5,500*

* Exemption is apportioned if there are several trusts created by the same settlor, but with each trust entitled to a minimum exemption of £1,110 for 2015/16, £1,100 for 2014/15.

INHERITANCE TAX	Deaths after 5/4/2012
Threshold / Nil-rate band	£325,000
Death rate	40%
Lower death rate (10% or more given to charity)	36%
Chargeable lifetime transfers rate	20%

VAT	2015/16
Standard rate	20%
Reduced rate	5%
Registration threshold after 31.3.2015 (previously £81,000 after 31.3.2014)	£82,000

NATIONAL INSURANCE	2015/16

(2014/15 in brackets where different)

Class 1 contributions

Not contracted-out

Employee contribution is 12% of earnings between £155 (£153) and £815 (£805) p.w. plus 2% of all earnings above £815 (£805) p.w. Between £112 (£111) and £155 (£153) p.w., no employee contributions are payable but a notional contribution is deemed to have been paid to protect contributory benefit entitlement. Employer contribution is 13.8% of all earnings in excess of the first £156 (£153) p.w. For 2015/16, employer contribution is reduced to 0% of earnings between £156 and £815 p.w. if employee is under 21. Most employers can claim employment allowance of up to £2,000 a year against their liability for employer contributions.

Contracted-out

The 'not contracted-out' rates for employees in salary-related schemes are reduced on the band of earnings from £112 (£111) p.w. to £770 p.w. by 1.4%. For the employer, they are reduced on the same band of earnings by 3.4%.

Class 1A and 1B contributions	13.8%
Class 2 contributions	
Flat weekly rate	£2.80 (£2.75)
Exemption limit	£5,965 (£5,885)
Class 3 contributions	
Flat weekly rate	£14.10 (£13.90)
Class 4 contributions	

9% on the band of profits between £8,061 (£7,956) and £42,385 (£41,865) plus 2% on all profits above £42,385 (£41,865).

Administration of Tax

Digital Tax Accounts

The Government will abolish the tax return for millions of individuals and small business through the introduction of digital tax accounts. A roadmap setting out the policy and administrative changes will be published later this year. In addition, the Government will consult on a new payment process to support the use of digital tax accounts that allow tax and National Insurance contributions to be collected outside of PAYE and self-assessment. This will be legislated for in the next Parliament.

Direct Recovery of Debts due to HMRC from Debtors' Bank and Building Society Accounts

HMRC will be able to collect payment of tax and duties directly from credit balances in debtors' bank and building society accounts, including ISAs, without first having to apply to the courts. HMRC will only take action against debtors who owe over £1,000 of tax or tax credits. They will always leave a minimum aggregate of £5,000 across debtors' accounts, and will only put a hold on funds up to the value of the debt. Secondary legislation to be published shortly will set out details of the process and safeguards for taxpayers.

The Government intends to legislate this measure in a future Finance Bill.

HMRC Tax Enquiries – Closure Rules

The Government has consulted on a proposal to introduce a new power, enabling HMRC to refer matters to the tax tribunal with a view to achieving early resolution of one or more aspects of a tax enquiry, whilst leaving other aspects of the tax enquiry open. The Government is currently considering the consultation responses.

UK's Automatic Exchange of Information Agreements

In compliance with the UK's obligations to improve international tax compliance, regulations will be introduced to create due diligence and reporting obligations for UK financial institutions. With effect from 1 January 2016, the obligations will require financial institutions to:

- identify accounts maintained for account holders who are tax resident in jurisdictions with which the UK has entered into an agreement to exchange to help tackle tax evasion; and
- collect and report information to HMRC.

The regulations also revoke and replace the current implementing regulations for the UK's exchange of information agreement with the USA (FATCA). These new regulations will have effect 21 days from the date that they are laid.

Personal Taxation

Basic Personal Allowance and Transferable Allowance for 2015/16

The personal allowance for those born after 5 April 1938 will be £10,600 for 2015/16. As a corollary, the transferable allowance for married couples and civil partners (10% of the personal allowance) will be £1,060. The higher rate threshold (i.e. the aggregate of the personal allowance and the basic rate limit) will be £42,385.

Personal Allowance and Basic Rate Limit for 2016/17 and 2017/18

The personal allowance will be £10,800 and £11,000 for 2016/17 and 2017/18 respectively. As a consequence there will no longer be a separate age-related allowance for 2016/17 onwards. The basic rate limit will be £31,900 for 2016/17 and £32,300 for 2017/18. The combined effect is that the higher rate threshold will be £42,700 in 2016/17 and £43,300 in 2017/18.

Charge for using Remittance Basis

An individual not domiciled in the UK who chooses to be taxed on the remittance basis on overseas income and chargeable gains must pay a special additional tax charge. This is currently £30,000 if the individual has been UK resident in at least 7 of the 9 preceding tax years or £50,000 if he has been UK resident in at least 12 of the 14 preceding years. For 2015/16 onwards the £50,000 charge is to increase to £60,000. The £30,000 charge will remain unchanged. The additional charge will be increased to a new level of £90,000 if the individual has been UK resident in at least 17 of the 20 preceding tax years.

Exemption from Income Tax for the Bereavement Support Payment

With effect from a date to be announced, the bereavement support payment (BSP) will replace the current bereavement allowance, bereavement payment and widowed parent's allowance for bereaved people who lose their spouse or civil partner. Once in payment, BSP will be exempt from income tax.

Miscellaneous Loss Relief for Income Tax

Anti-avoidance legislation will deny a person miscellaneous loss relief for income tax purposes where a loss arises as a result of tax avoidance arrangements. The legislation will also deny miscellaneous loss relief against miscellaneous income that arises as a result of tax avoidance arrangements. This is effective for losses and income arising on and after 3 December 2014.

In addition, for 2015/16 onwards, the offset of a miscellaneous loss will be limited to miscellaneous income that is chargeable to income tax under, or by virtue of, the same provision as that under which the loss would have been chargeable had it been profits or other income instead of a loss.

Bad Debt Relief on Peer-to-peer Lending

Individuals who make loans through peer-to-peer (P2P) platforms will be able to offset bad debts arising against the interest they receive from P2P loans when calculating their taxable income. These changes will have effect for loans made from 6 April 2015, but the legislation will be in a future Finance Bill.

Employment Taxation

Abolition of the £8,500 Threshold for Benefits in Kind

The £8,500 earnings threshold that determines whether employees pay income tax on all of their benefits in kind and expenses, and whether employers pay Class 1A National Insurance contributions (NICs), is to be abolished for 2016/17 onwards.

Currently, an employee in so-called lower-paid employment (i.e. whose earnings for the tax year are less than £8,500) pays tax only on certain employee benefits, e.g. living accommodation, vouchers and credit-tokens. The abolition of the threshold will mean all employees will be taxed on their benefits and expenses in the same way. The employer's NICs treatment will follow the income tax treatment.

New exemptions will be introduced to cover benefits for ministers of religion earning less than £8,500 and for employees who are carers; the latter will cover board and lodging on a reasonable scale that is provided in the home of the person being cared for.

Statutory Exemption for Trivial Benefits in Kind

A statutory exemption is to be introduced for 2015/16 onwards that will allow employers to identify and treat certain low value benefits provided to employees or former employees as trivial. These benefits will then be exempt from income tax and Class 1A National Insurance contributions and will not need to be reported to HMRC. A benefit will be trivial if it meets all the following conditions:

- the benefit is not cash or a cash voucher;
- the cost of providing it does not exceed £50;
- the benefit is not provided under salary sacrifice arrangements or any other contractual obligation; and

- it is not provided in recognition of particular services performed, or to be performed, by the employee.

An annual cap of £300 will be introduced for office holders of close companies (broadly those controlled by 5 or fewer people) and employees who are family members of those office holders. Those affected by this cap will be able to receive a maximum of £300 worth of exempt trivial benefits each year.

Employee Expenses: Dispensations

The current system whereby an employer can apply to HMRC for a dispensation to pay expenses free of tax in certain circumstances will be scrapped for 2016/17 onwards. Instead, expenses provided to employees will automatically be exempt in any case where the employee would have been eligible for a deduction had he incurred and paid the equivalent expense himself. The exemption will also allow the employee to be paid a scale rate rather than be reimbursed the actual expense he has incurred. This can either be a rate set by HMRC or a rate that the employer has agreed with HMRC. The exemption will also apply to benefits in kind provided by employers in respect of expenses incurred by their employees. It will not apply to expenses/benefits provided as part of a salary sacrifice arrangement or in conjunction with other arrangements that seek to replace salary with expenses. Similar rules will apply for NIC purposes.

Collection of Tax on Benefits and Expenses through Voluntary Payrolling

Legislation is to be introduced to allow HMRC to make changes to the PAYE Regulations to provide for voluntary payrolling of certain benefits in kind. The intention is that employers will be able to opt to payroll benefits for cars, car fuel, medical insurance and gym membership for 2016/17 onwards. Where employers do so, they will not have to make a return on Form P11D for these benefits. Instead, they will report the value of the benefits through Real Time Information, and that value will count as PAYE income liable to deduction using the PAYE Tax Tables. The amended Regulations will determine the value to be placed on the benefit for this purpose.

Van Benefit Charge for Zero Emission Vans

The van benefit charge for zero emission vans will increase from £nil, beginning in 2015/16. The van benefit charge for such vans will be 20% of the van benefit charge for vans which emit CO_2 in 2015/16, 40% in 2016/17, 60% in 2017/18, 80% in 2018/19 and 90% in 2019/20. From 2020/21, the van benefit charge for zero emission vans will be the same as the van benefit charge for vans which emit CO_2.

Company Car Tax Rates and Bands for 2017/18 and 2018/19

Rates and bands for 2017/18

For cars with CO_2 emissions there will be a 9% band for emissions of 0g–50g CO_2 per km, a 13% band for emissions of 51g–75g CO_2 per km, a 17% band for other low emission cars (76g–94g CO_2 per km); and a 1% increase for each rise in emissions of 5g CO_2 per kg from 95g CO_2 (18%) to the existing maximum of 37%.

For cars without a CO_2 emissions figure the appropriate percentage for a cylinder capacity of up to 1,400cc will be 18%; for 1,401–2,000cc it will be 29%; and for 2,000cc plus it will remain at 37%.

For cars first registered before 1 January 1998 the appropriate percentage for capacity up to 1,400cc will be 18%; for 1,401–2,000cc it will be 29%; and for more than 2,000cc it will remain at 37%.

Rates and bands for 2018/19

For cars with CO_2 emissions there will be a 13% band for emissions of 0g–50g CO_2 per km, a 16% band for emissions of 51g–75g CO_2 per km, a 19% band for emissions of 76g–94g CO_2 per km; and a 1% increase for each rise of 5g CO_2 per km from 95g CO_2 (20%) to the existing maximum of 37%.

For cars without a CO_2 emissions figure, the appropriate percentage for a cylinder capacity of up to 1,400cc will be 20%; for 1,401–2,000cc it will be 31%; and for more than 2,000cc it will remain at 37%.

For cars first registered before 1 January 1998 the appropriate percentage for capacity of up to 1,400cc will be 20%; for 1,401–2,000 cc it will be 31%; and for more than 2,000cc it will remain at 37%.

Employment Intermediaries

The Government is concerned at the growing use of overarching contracts of employment that allow some temporary workers and their employers to benefit from tax relief for home-to-work travel expenses, relief not generally available to other workers. The rules will be changed to restrict travel and subsistence relief for workers engaged through an employment intermediary, such as an umbrella company or a personal service company, and under the supervision, direction and control of the end-user. This will take effect from 6 April 2016 following consultation on the detail.

Exemption from Income Tax and National Insurance Contributions (NICs): Lump Sums provided under Armed Forces Early Departure Scheme

Lump sum payments made to qualifying armed forces personnel under the existing Early Departure Payment (EDP) 2005 scheme are exempt from income tax and are disregarded for NICs purposes. The scheme will be replaced by the EDP 2015 scheme on 1 April 2015. Legislation will be introduced in Finance Bill 2015 to ensure that the tax and NICs treatment of lump sum payments under the new scheme is the same as those under the existing scheme.

National Insurance Contributions

NICs for the Self-Employed

Class 2 contributions will be abolished in the next Parliament. Class 4 contributions will be reformed to introduce a new contributory benefit test. The Government intends to consult on the proposals later in 2015.

Business Tax

Farmers' Averaging

The period over which self-employed farmers can average their profits for income tax purposes is to be increased from 2 to 5 years with effect from 6 April 2016.

Simplified Expenses: Partnerships

The government will amend the simplified expenses regime introduced in FA 2013 to ensure that partnerships can fully access the provisions in respect of the use of a home and where business premises are also a home.

Tax Relief for Businesses Contributing to a Partnership Funding Flood Defence Scheme

Finance Bill 2015 will introduce legislation to allow a specific income tax or corporation tax deduction from business profits or property business profits for contributions made on or after 1 January 2015 to partnership funding schemes for flood defence projects (known as Flood and Coastal Erosion Risk Management (FCERM) projects). No deduction will be allowed if the contributor, or a person connected with him, receives, or is entitled to receive, a disqualifying benefit.

Capital Allowances

Extension of Enhanced Capital Allowances for Zero-Emission Goods Vehicles to 2018

Legislation will be introduced in Finance Bill 2015 to extend the availability of 100% enhanced capital allowances (ECAs) for zero-emission goods vehicles to 31 March 2018 for corporation tax purposes and to 5 April 2018 for income tax purposes. In addition a rule will be introduced preventing claims to the ECA being made if another form of State aid has been, or will be, received, in order to bring the relief into line with other State aids.

Capital Allowances: Anti-Avoidance Rules for Plant and Machinery

With effect from 26 February 2015 a further restriction will apply to the amount of qualifying expenditure on which capital allowances may be claimed on an item of plant and machinery as a result of a connected party transaction, a sale and leaseback, a transfer and long funding leaseback, or a transfer and subsequent hire-purchase. The new restriction will apply in certain circumstances where the person disposing of the asset does not bring a disposal value into account. When the restriction applies the person acquiring the asset will be treated, for the purposes of plant and machinery allowances, as having no qualifying expenditure.

Corporation Tax

Diverted Profits Tax

The diverted profits tax will apply to diverted profits arising on or after 1 April 2015, with apportionment rules for accounting periods that straddle that date. The tax does not apply where, broadly, the parties to the relevant transactions are small and medium sized enterprises. It is a tax that is aimed at large multinational groups of companies and is intended to deter the implementation of aggressive tax planning which seeks to divert profits away from the UK, in order to minimise the group's overall corporation tax bill.

The diverted profits tax effectively operates by applying a 25% tax charge on diverted profits relating to UK activity and applies to companies that:

- design their activities to avoid creating a taxable presence (a permanent establishment) in the UK; or
- create a tax advantage by using transactions or entities that lack economic substance. Note this rule also applies where a non-UK resident company ('the foreign company') trades through a UK permanent establishment.

The initial onus to notify liability falls on the relevant company.

Film Tax Relief

Subject to State aid clearance, the Government will increase the rate of film tax relief to 25% for all qualifying expenditure. This will apply from 1 April 2015 or, if later, the date of approval by the European Commission.

High-end Television Tax Relief

With effect for qualifying expenditure incurred on and after 1 April 2015, subject to State aid clearance, the minimum UK expenditure requirement for television tax relief will be reduced from 25% to 10% for companies within the charge to corporation tax that are directly involved in the production of high-end television or animation. The cultural test will be modernised.

Children's Television Tax Relief

The existing television tax reliefs for animation and high-end TV are extended to children's television programmes, including children's game shows and competitions. Companies within the charge to corporation tax that are directly involved in the production of children's television programmes will be able to claim a deduction from their profits at the rate of 25% on qualifying expenditure incurred on eligible programmes on and after 1 April 2015. Where that additional deduction results in a loss, the company may surrender the loss for a payable tax credit. Both the additional deduction and the payable credit are calculated on the basis of a maximum of 80% of the total UK core expenditure by the qualifying company. The additional deduction is 100% of qualifying core expenditure and the payable tax credit is 25% of losses surrendered.

Children's programming will not be subject to the £1m per programme hour threshold or the 30 minute slot length that apply to high-end TV programmes.

Orchestra Tax Relief

Legislation will be introduced in a future Finance Bill for a new relief for orchestras at a rate of 25% on qualifying expenditure from 1 April 2016.

Accelerated Payments and Group Relief

The Government will introduce legislation to ensure that the accelerated payments legislation works effectively where avoidance arrangements give rise to losses surrendered as group relief. It will be applicable to all cases involving group relief where there is an open enquiry or open appeal on or after the day of Royal Assent to Finance Act 2015. Where a company makes a return asserting a tax advantage from chosen arrangements, and then surrenders all or part of that advantage as group relief, the legislation will allow HMRC to issue an accelerated payment notice to the effect that the asserted advantage may not be surrendered while the dispute is in progress.

Modernisation of Corporate Debt and Derivative Contracts

A series of wide-ranging changes have been announced to update, simplify and rationalise the legislation on corporate debt and derivative contracts.

The main changes will be:

- The relationship between accountancy and tax will be clarified and strengthened. In particular, the requirement that amounts brought into account for tax must 'fairly represent' the profits, gains and losses arising will be removed.
- The calculation of taxable amounts will be amended to bring them into line with the usual approach to the computation of profits. Taxation will be based only on amounts recognised as items of accounting profit or loss, rather than on amounts recognised anywhere in accounts – in reserves or equity, for example. A transitional rule will ensure that this change is broadly tax neutral.
- Taxable amounts that would otherwise arise where arrangements are made to restructure the debts of a company in financial distress with a view to ensuring its continued solvency will be excluded. This will cover situations where debt is released, or where the terms are modified, supplementing and extending the existing rule that exempts credits arising in debtor companies when creditors exchange debt investment for an equity stake.
- A new regime-wide anti-avoidance rule will counter arrangements entered into with a main purpose of obtaining a tax advantage by way of the loan relationships or derivative contracts rules. As a consequence, a number of existing specific anti-avoidance rules will be repealed.

The first two changes will apply for accounting periods commencing on or after 1 January 2016. The latter two apply, respectively, to releases and modifications on or after 1 January 2015 and arrangements entered into on or after 1 April 2015. The Government has announced that these changes will be legislated for in a future Finance Bill.

Research and Development

Legislation will be introduced to restrict qualifying expenditure for research and development (R&D) tax credits so that the cost of consumable items incorporated in products that are sold in the normal course of a company's business are not eligible for R&D relief, with effect from 1 April 2015. Qualifying expenditure on consumable items will be limited to the cost of only those items fully used up or expended by the R&D activity itself which do not go on to be sold as part of a commercial product. This restriction will not apply where the product of the R&D is transferred as waste, or where it is transferred but no consideration is given.

In addition, from 1 April 2015, the rate of the above the line credit for large companies will increase from 10% to 11% and the rate of the relief for the SME scheme will increase from 225% to 230%.

Consortium Relief

Legislation will be introduced to repeal all requirements relating to the location of a 'link company' for consortium claims to group relief. This will apply to all claims to group relief for accounting periods beginning on and after 10 December 2014. Prior to this amendment the link company had to be in the UK or EEA. This measure makes the tax system simpler by removing differences in treatment of link companies based in the UK and other jurisdictions.

Goodwill Transfers on Incorporation

Corporation tax relief will be restricted where a company acquires internally-generated goodwill and customer-related intangible assets from related individuals on the incorporation of a business on or after 3 December 2014, unless the transfer is made pursuant to an unconditional obligation entered into before that date. Currently companies are given corporation tax relief on internally-generated goodwill even when there is continuing economic ownership. This change will ensure that businesses that do not incorporate are not at a disadvantage compared to those which do.

Companies already receiving relief for goodwill recognised on incorporation will not be affected.

Corporate Loss Refresh Prevention

From 18 March 2015 there are restrictions to prevent companies converting brought forward trading losses, non-trading loan relationship deficits and management expenses into in-year deductions. Where a company enters into an arrangement, the main purpose of which is to utilise the brought forward losses, it will be unable to use the brought forward losses against profits created as a result of the arrangement.

Deduction at Source from Interest Paid on Private Placements

A UK company's duty to deduct income tax from certain payments of yearly interest will not apply to a payment of interest on qualifying private placements and the condition relating to the minimum term of the security will be removed. The primary legislation for this measure will have effect on or after the date of Royal Assent to Finance Act 2015 and regulations will set out detailed conditions of private placements that qualify for the exemption. These regulations may allow the exemption to be targeted at particular types of company, and may contain safeguards to ensure the exemption is not abused.

Country-by-country Reporting

Legislation will be introduced in Finance Bill 2015 that gives the UK the power to implement the OECD model for country-by-country reporting. The new rules will require multi-national enterprises (MNEs) with a parent company in the UK to make an annual country-by-country report to HMRC showing, for each tax jurisdiction in which they do business:

- the amount of revenue, profit before income tax and income tax paid and accrued; and
- their total employment, capital, retained earnings and tangible assets.

Regulations giving effect to the scope and detail of the reporting obligation will be made at a later date.

Late Paid Interest

As part of the review of the legislation on corporate debt announced at Budget 2013, the Government will repeal rules concerning loans made to UK companies by a connected company in a non-qualifying territory.

Banks

Bank Levy Rate Increase

Legislation in Finance Bill 2015 will increase the rate of the bank levy to 0.21% from 1 April 2015. A proportionate increase to 0.105% will be made to the half rate from the same date.

Capital Gains Tax

Non-UK Residents and UK Residential Property

Capital gains tax will be charged on gains accruing to non-UK resident persons on disposals of UK residential property made on or after 6 April 2015. This will affect:

- non-UK resident individuals;

- non-UK resident trusts;
- personal representatives of a deceased person who was non-UK resident; and
- non-UK resident companies controlled by five or fewer persons, except where the company itself, or at least one of the controlling persons, is a 'qualifying institutional investor'.

It will also affect some UK resident individuals disposing of properties overseas or who spend part of a tax year abroad.

Tax will be due for payment within 30 days of the property being conveyed, unless the person has a current self-assessment record with HMRC, when payment will be at the normal due date for the tax year in which the disposal is made.

In addition, private residence relief (PRR) will be restricted where a property is located in a jurisdiction in which a taxpayer is not resident. In these circumstances, the property will only be capable of being regarded as the person's main residence for PRR purposes for a tax year where the person meets a 90-day test for time spent in the property over the year.

Entrepreneurs' Relief on Deferred Gains

Finance Act 2015 will allow gains that are eligible for entrepreneurs' relief (ER), but which are instead deferred into investments that qualify for the Enterprise Investment Scheme (EIS) or Social Investment Tax Relief (SITR), to remain eligible for ER when the gain is realised. This will benefit qualifying gains on disposals that would be eligible for ER but are deferred into EIS or SITR on or after 3 December 2014.

Entrepreneurs' Relief for Disposals of Goodwill

Legislation in Finance Bill 2015 will prevent entrepreneurs' relief from being available on disposals of goodwill on or after 3 December 2014 to a close limited company to which the seller is related. The relief may still be claimed by partners in a firm who do not hold or acquire any stake in the successor company.

Restricting Entrepreneurs' Relief on Associated Disposals

The rules relating to entrepreneurs' relief on associated disposals are to be amended. For disposals on or after 18 March 2015, in order to qualify for the relief on a disposal of a privately-owned asset, the claimant must reduce his participation in the business by also disposing of a minimum 5% of the shares of the company carrying on the business, or (where the business is carried on in partnership) of a minimum 5% share in the assets of the partnership carrying on the business.

Entrepreneurs' Relief, Joint Ventures and Partnerships

Legislation is to be introduced to ensure that those who benefit from entrepreneurs' relief have a 5% directly-held shareholding in a genuine trading company. For disposals on or after 18 March 2015, the definitions of a 'trading company' and 'the holding company of a trading group' do not take account of activities carried on by joint venture companies which a company is invested in, or of partnerships of which a company is a member. Therefore a company would need to have a significant trade of its own in order to be considered as a trading company.

Exemption for Certain Wasting Assets

Legislation will be introduced to make it clear that the capital gains tax wasting asset exemption applies only if the person selling the asset has used it as plant in their own business as opposed to its being used as plant in another person's business. This change will have effect for gains accruing on and after 1 April 2015 for corporation tax purposes and 6 April 2015 for CGT purposes.

Threshold amount for ATED-related Capital Gains Tax

Legislation will be introduced in Finance Bill 2015 to reduce the threshold amount for consideration received on a disposal of residential property, above which an Annual Tax on Enveloped Dwellings (ATED)-related gain may accrue. The threshold will fall from £2m to £1m for disposals on or after 6 April 2015, and then to £500,000 for disposals on or after 6 April 2016.

Savings and Investments

Personal Savings Allowance

It is proposed that a new Personal Savings Allowance be introduced from 6 April 2016. For a basic rate taxpayer, this will exempt from income tax the first £1,000 of savings income, such as bank and building society interest. For a higher rate taxpayer, only the first £500 will be exempted. The Personal Savings Allowance will not be available to additional rate taxpayers. At the same time, the deduction of basic rate tax at source from interest paid by banks and building societies will be abolished for all savers.

Individual Savings Accounts (ISAs)

It is announced that regulations will be introduced in Autumn 2015 to enable a cash ISA investor to withdraw money from his ISA and pay it back in again during the same tax year without the second transaction counting towards his ISA subscription limit for that year. Regulations will also be introduced to extend the list of qualifying investments for ISAs and Child Trust Funds.

Help to Buy ISAs

This proposed scheme for first-time home buyers will provide a bonus to each person who has saved into a Help to Buy Individual Savings Account. The bonus will be paid at the time the savings are used to purchase a home. For every £200 saved, the Government will provide a £50 bonus up to a maximum of £3,000 on £12,000 of savings. Accounts are expected to be available through banks and building societies from Autumn 2015. Savers will be able to make an initial deposit of £1,000 and a monthly saving of up to £200. The bonus will be available on home purchases of up to £450,000 in London and up to £250,000 elsewhere in the UK.

Special Purpose Share Schemes

Companies sometimes use special purpose share schemes (often called 'B share schemes') to offer shareholders the option to receive, instead of a dividend, a similar amount via an issue of new shares. The shares issued are subsequently purchased by the company or are sold to a pre-arranged third party. Under legislation to be introduced, any amount thus received by a shareholder after 5 April 2015 will be charged to income tax by treating it as a distribution, i.e. a dividend, made to the shareholder by the company in the tax year in which it is received. It will qualify for a dividend tax credit to the same extent that an actual distribution by the company to the shareholder would have qualified.

The above will apply whenever a company has given a shareholder the option to receive, instead of a dividend, something that would not be subject to income tax, and the shareholder has taken that option. If at any time a tax other than income tax (e.g. capital gains tax) is charged in relation to the receipt, then in order to avoid a double charge to tax, the recipient may make a claim for consequential adjustments to be made in respect of the other tax.

Social Investment Tax Relief – Enlarging the Scheme

Subject to EU State aid clearance, the maximum amount that can be invested through Social Investment Tax Relief will be increased, and the range of qualifying social enterprises broadened to include certain small horticulture and agriculture projects that will no longer qualify for subsidy as a result of the forthcoming Common Agricultural Policy reforms. The range of eligible social impact bonds (SIBs) will also be widened to include certain spot purchased and sub-contracted SIBs.

There will be a consultation on allowing investments to be made indirectly, through a social investment form of a venture capital trust scheme, a 'Social VCT'.

Social Venture Capital Trusts

The Government will legislate for Social Venture Capital Trusts (VCTs) in a future Finance Bill. The rate of income tax relief for investment in Social VCTs will be set at 30%, subject to State aid clearance. Investors will pay no tax on dividends received from a Social VCT or capital gains tax on disposals of shares in a Social VCT. Social VCTs will have the same excluded activities as the Social Investment Tax Relief Scheme.

Changes to Venture Capital Schemes for Companies and Community Organisations Benefiting from Energy Subsidies

From 6 April 2015, companies and community organisations will cease to be eligible for the Seed Enterprise Investment Scheme (SEIS), Enterprise Investment Scheme (EIS) and Venture Capital Trust (VCT) Scheme where their activities consist wholly or substantially of the subsidised generation or export of electricity, or the subsidised generation of heat or production of gas or fuel, and:

- the activities are carried out by community groups; or
- where anaerobic digestion or hydroelectric power is involved; or
- the company has entered into a Contract for Difference under the Energy Act 2013.

For Social Investment Tax Relief (SITR), activities that are subsidised by way of Feed-in Tariffs will cease to be excluded activities following State aid clearance of the scheme. As a transitional measure, the provisions excluding community energy organisations from EIS, SEIS and VCT will take effect six months after approval for the extension of SITR.

SEIS, EIS and VCT changes

It is intended that the Enterprise Investment Scheme, Seed Enterprise Investment Scheme and Venture Capital Trust Scheme will be amended, subject to State aid approval, so that:

- companies must be less than 12 years old when receiving their first EIS or VCT investment, unless that investment will lead to a substantial change in activity;
- a cap for all schemes will be introduced of £15m, increasing to £20m for knowledge-intensive companies; and
- there will be an increase in the employee limit for knowledge-intensive companies from 249 to 499.

With effect from 6 April 2015, the requirement that 70% of SEIS money must be spent before EIS or VCT funding can be raised will be removed.

Inheritance Tax

Relevant Property Trusts

Following the Government's consultation on proposals for changes to the inheritance tax regime for relevant property trusts, a number of measures are to be included in a future Finance Bill:

- In calculating the rate of inheritance tax for the purposes of the ten-year charge and the exit charge, the requirement to include certain property that is not relevant property is removed for charges arising on or after 6 April 2015.
- A new rule is introduced, subject to transitional provisions, for ten-year anniversary charges, exit charges and charges on 18/25 trusts arising on or after 6 April 2015. Where property of more than £5,000 is added to two or more relevant property settlements on the same day (and after the commencement of those settlements), then, in calculating the rate of tax for any of those settlements, the value of the property so added to the other settlements, together with the value of property added to those settlements at the date of their commencement, must be brought into account in calculating the rate of tax.
- The requirement that a claim for conditional exemption must be made and the property designated as heritage property before the ten-year charge is removed so that, for ten-year charges that would otherwise arise on or after the date of Royal Assent to the Finance Act in which the legislation is included, the claim for designation can be made within the two years following the date of the ten-year anniversary.
- The rules applying to settlements made before 22 March 2006 that give an interest in possession to the settlor or their spouse or civil partner (or surviving spouse or civil partner) are amended. Where, on or after the day after the date of Royal Assent to the Finance Act in which the legislation is included, one party to the couple succeeds to the interest in possession of the other, the settled property will then come within the relevant property trusts regime unless the successor's interest is an immediate post-death interest, a disabled person's interest or a transitional serial interest.
- For deaths on or after 10 December 2014, where property is left in a relevant property trust and an appointment is made of that property to the spouse or civil partner of the testator, that appointment is read back into the will and exemption from inheritance tax can apply even where the appointment is made in the three months following death.

Exemption for Emergency Service Personnel and Humanitarian Aid Workers

Effective for deaths on or after 19 March 2014, IHT will not be charged on the estates of emergency service personnel and humanitarian aid workers whose death has been caused directly or hastened by injury or illness while responding to emergency circumstances. The Government has clarified that the exemption applies to serving and former police officers and service personnel targeted because of their status.

Extending Exemption for Medals and Other Awards

The exclusion from inheritance tax that applies to medals and other decorations that are awarded for valour and gallantry is extended to all decorations and medals awarded by the Crown or by another country or territory outside the UK to the armed forces, emergency service personnel and to individuals in recognition of their achievements and service in public life. The extension is effective in relation to transfers of value made or treated as made on or after 3 December 2014.

Interest Changes to Support the New Digital Service

Legislation will be introduced in a future Finance Bill to provide for a new inheritance tax online service. Draft regulations to facilitate the use of electronic communications will be published shortly after the Budget. It was announced at Autumn Statement that future regulations would also update the instalment interest provisions relating to certain financial institutions and companies, and clarify the period from when interest is charged. The amendments will come into force on an appointed day to be specified in regulations. This is expected to be at the same time as the new online service becomes available.

Charities

Gift Aid Intermediaries

A non-charity intermediary will be able to submit a gift aid declaration on behalf of a donor, and the recipient charity able to claim gift aid on the basis of such a declaration. Primary legislation will be effective from Royal Assent to Finance Act 2015 with further details governing the declarations introduced in later regulations.

Gift Aid Small Donations Scheme

From 6 April 2016 the maximum annual donation amount that can be claimed by a charity under the Gift Aid Small Donations Scheme will be increased to £8,000, thus enabling the charity to claim a Gift Aid style top-up payment from HMRC of up to £2,000.

Status of Certain Bodies for Tax Purposes

The Commonwealth War Graves Commission (CWGC) and the Imperial War Graves Endowment Fund (which provides investment income for the CWGC) will be treated as charities for tax purposes from the date of Royal Assent to Finance Act 2015.

Pensions

Reduction in Lifetime Allowance

It is intended to introduce legislation in the next Parliament to reduce the pension lifetime allowance from 6 April 2016 from £1.25m to £1m, accompanied by fixed and individual protection arrangements. From 2018 the allowance will rise in line with the consumer prices index.

Annuity Flexibility

It is intended to introduce legislation in a future Finance Bill, to be effective from April 2016, to allow those already in receipt of an annuity to sell to a third party and take the proceeds directly or draw them down over a number of years. Income tax would be at the individual's marginal rate.

Taxation of Inherited Annuities

From 6 April 2015, beneficiaries of individuals who die under the age of 75 with a joint life or guaranteed term annuity will be able to receive any future payments from such policies tax-free where no payments have been made to the beneficiary before 6 April 2015. The tax rules will also be changed to allow joint life annuities to be paid to any beneficiary. Where the individual was over 75, the beneficiary will pay their marginal rate of income tax.

Anti-avoidance

Disclosure of Tax Avoidance Schemes Regime Changes

The disclosure of tax avoidance schemes (DOTAS) regime is amended to:

- ensure disclosure is made by persons resident in the UK where a promoter not resident in the UK fails to disclose;
- change the information that must be provided to HMRC;
- enable HMRC to publish information about promoters and disclosed schemes; and
- establish a taskforce to enforce the strengthened regime.

Changes to primary legislation included in the Finance Bill come into force on the date of Royal Assent, and further amendments will be made through secondary legislation and will come into force at a later date. The changes will be extended to schemes avoiding National Insurance contributions.

Promoters of Tax Avoidance Schemes

The following changes will be made in a future Finance Bill to the legislation that affects high-risk promoters of avoidance schemes:

- HMRC will be able to issue conduct notices to a broader range of connected persons;
- the time limit for issuing notices to promoters who have failed to disclose avoidance schemes to HMRC under DOTAS is amended;
- a new threshold condition will be introduced for failing to comply with NICs disclosure requirements; and
- the threshold conditions will take account of decisions by independent bodies in matters relating to professional misconduct.

Serial Avoiders

Legislation will be included in a future Finance Bill to introduce tougher measures for those who persistently enter into tax avoidance schemes which fail. These will include a special reporting requirement and a surcharge on any such serial avoider whose latest tax return is inaccurate as a result of a further failed scheme. The Government will look to restrict access to reliefs for serial avoiders and to name and shame them. Legislation will be introduced in due course to widen the scope of the current disclosure regime by including promoters whose schemes regularly fail.

GAAR Penalties

Legislation will be introduced in a future Finance Bill that will increase the deterrent effect of the General Anti-Abuse Rule (GAAR), by introducing a specific, tax-geared penalty that applies to cases tackled by the GAAR.

Penalties for Offshore Non-compliance

The penalty for failure to notify chargeability to income tax or capital gains tax, the late filing penalty for self-assessment tax returns and the penalty for careless or deliberate errors in documents is currently in each case increased where the failure involves an offshore matter. This offshore penalty regime is to be strengthened and extended with effect from 1 April 2016 so that it will:

- apply additionally to inheritance tax;
- cover cases where the proceeds of domestic non-compliance are situated or held outside the UK; and
- have four (increased from three) levels of penalty, with the lowest level applying to countries that adopt automatic exchange of information.

On and after the date of Royal Assent to Finance Act 2015 there will be a new and additional penalty where:

- a person is liable to one of the penalties mentioned above;
- that penalty is for a deliberate failure;
- assets are moved from a specified country to a non-specified country; and

- a main purpose of the movement is to prevent or delay the discovery by HMRC of the potential loss of revenue giving rise to the said penalty.

Countries will be specified for this purpose if they have committed to exchanging information.

Disclosure Facilities

The following have been announced in relation to current disclosure facilities:

- the disclosure period of the Liechtenstein Disclosure Facility will be shortened, with the end date being changed from April 2016 to December 2015; and
- the disclosure period of the Crown Dependencies Disclosure Facility will also be shortened, with the end date being changed from September 2016 to December 2015.

A new time-limited disclosure facility will be introduced that will run after the existing facilities close, with tougher terms than existing facilities, including penalties of at least 30% and no guarantee around criminal investigation.

Stamp and Property Taxes

Stamp Duty Land Tax: Extension of Multiple Dwellings Relief

The SDLT relief for transactions involving interests in more than one dwelling is to be extended to include purchases from certain shared ownership bodies of superior leasehold interests in property subject to shared ownership leases where the transaction is part of a lease and leaseback arrangement. The change will apply to transactions with an effective date on or after the date of Royal Assent to Finance Act 2015.

Stamp Duty Land Tax: Alternative Property Finance

A change is to be made to the SDLT alternative property finance reliefs which apply where a property is purchased using a method of financing which does not involve the payment of interest. The reliefs will be extended to apply to all purchases which are financed using a home purchase plan provided by an authorised provider. The change will apply to transactions with an effective date on or after the date of Royal Assent to Finance Act 2015.

Annual Tax on Enveloped Dwellings (ATED)

The 2015/16 ATED annual charges will be as follows:

Property value	Annual charge in 2015/16
More than £1m but not more than £2m	£7,000
More than £2m but not more than £5m	£23,350
More than £5m but not more than £10m	£54,450
More than £10m but not more than £20m	£109,050
More than £20m	£218,200

Reducing Administrative Burden of ATED

Legislation will be introduced in Finance Bill 2015 to reduce the administrative burden on businesses which hold properties eligible for a relief from ATED and for which there is no tax liability. For chargeable periods beginning on or after 1 April 2015 such businesses will be able to submit a relief declaration return.

A relief declaration return can only relate to one type of ATED relief, but subject to this it can be made in respect of one or more single-dwelling interests, which do not need to be identified. For the 2015/16 year only, relief declaration returns must be filed by 1 October 2015. For subsequent years the normal filing date of 30 April will apply.

Value Added Tax

VAT Registration Thresholds

With effect from 1 April 2015, the VAT registration threshold will be increased from £81,000 to £82,000. The deregistration threshold will be increased from £79,000 to £80,000. The registration and deregistration thresholds for acquisitions from other EU member states will be increased from £81,000 to £82,000.

VAT Deductions Relating to Foreign Branches

Following the CJEU decision in *Credit Lyonnais* amendments to the VAT Regulations will mean that:

- calculations of recoverable input tax using the partial exemption standard method must exclude supplies made by establishments outside the UK;
- calculations of recoverable input tax using a partial exemption special method must exclude supplies made by establishments outside the UK;

- the use-based calculation for 'out-of-country' supplies is limited to supplies made from establishments within the UK.

The changes will have effect from the first day of a business's longer period which commences on or after 1 August 2015.

Power to Make Refunds to Named Bodies

Government departments are permitted to obtain refunds of VAT which they incur in relation to non-business activities. However, this does not extend to non-departmental public bodies and similar arm's-length bodies.

A future Finance Act will provide that the Treasury may, by order, name any such bodies as 'specified bodies', with the result that they will be able to recover the VAT which they incur on non-business activities. The aim of the measure is to prevent VAT from being a disincentive to cost-sharing arrangements between such bodies, which currently give rise to irrecoverable VAT.

Any hope of a windfall by a specified body will, however, be short lived; since the recipient will be government-funded, the extent of the funding will be adjusted downwards to take account of the VAT which is now recoverable.

Oil and Gas

Oil and Gas Companies

A package of measures has been announced to reform the oil and gas fiscal regime as follows:

- from 1 January 2015, the rate of the supplementary charge payable in respect of profits from oil and gas production in the UK or on the UK Continental Shelf is reduced to 20%;
- for chargeable periods ending after 31 December 2015 the rate of petroleum revenue tax payable in respect of profits from oil and gas production is reduced to 35%;
- for qualifying pre-commencement expenditure incurred in accounting periods ending on or after 5 December 2013, the ring-fence expenditure supplement is extended from six to ten accounting periods and the extended ring fence expenditure supplement is removed;
- new allowances will be introduced which will remove an amount equal to 62.5% of investment/capital expenditure incurred by a company from its adjusted ring-fence profits which are subject to the supplementary charge.

Miscellaneous

Investment Managers: Disguised Fee Income

For 2015/16 onwards, where an individual provides investment management services for a collective investment scheme through an arrangement involving partnerships, then any sum received for those services (the 'disguised fee') will be treated as profits of a trade, unless already charged to income tax. This will have effect in relation to all disguised fees arising on or after 6 April 2015, whenever the arrangement is entered into. Sums will not be caught if they represent a return on investments by the managers or a return which varies by reference to profits on funds. An individual thus charged will be able to claim a consequential adjustment if at any time tax is charged under another tax provision in respect of the same fee. The consequential adjustment cannot exceed the lesser of the two charges.